YOU DESERVE SATISFACTION.

Each year, some 15 million cars are built and delivered to automobile dealerships throughout the United States. Of those sold, it is estimated that as many as 1 in 10 will develop mechanical difficulties which cannot be satisfactorily repaired. Until recently, consumers were virtually powerless to do much more than tolerate repeated repair attempts, associated inconveniences and, occassionally, beligerent service personnel.

That has all changed. Sweeping reforms have been written into tough laws which protect the consumer's right to a safe, relatively trouble-free automobile. The problem is, most consumers have no idea what their rights are, or how to exercise those rights to force proper repairs, or obtain a refund or replacement vehicle if repairs cannot be competed.

LEMON AID was written to help consumers fight back using knowledge, diplomacy, correct procedures, and the power afforded them in their state's Lemon Law. Now, there's no longer a need to get angry when it's so easy to get...satisfaction.

LEMON AID

**Exercising Your Rights
Under The Consumer Lemon Law**

By Richard L. Kaye

Copyright © 1991 by Richard L. Kaye

All rights reserved. No part of this book may be reproduced or utilized in any form or by any means, electronic or mechanical, including photocopying, recording or by any information storage and retrieval system, without permission in writing from TeleTravel Network, Inc., P.O. Box 606, Northbrook, Illinois 60065-0606, U.S.A.

Library of Congress Catalog Card Number: 90-070382

ISBN 0-9623644-2-8

This edition published and printed in the United States of America.

First printing: April, 1991

Thanks to my "California Connection" for your research and dedication to this book. Without you, it couldn't have been written.

Thanks to Paul for his late nights on the computer.

Table of Contents

Introduction .... Page 1

Chapter 1: Consumer/Manufacturer Relationships............ Page 3

Chapter 2: The Case of John T. Consumer..................... Page 7

Chapter 3: Warranties and Lemon Law Legislation........... Page 9

Chapter 4: Lemon Law Definition and Explanation........... Page 12

Chapter 5: Documenting Your Car's Repair History........... Page 19

Chapter 6: Resolving Complaints............................... Page 23

Chapter 7: Initiating Lemon Law Action........................ Page 28

Chapter 8: The Lemon Law Process............................ Page 34

Appendix I: State Lemon Laws .... Page I-1

Appendix II: Manufacturer Contact Information............... Page II-1

Appendix III: Other Contact Information .... Page III-1

Index

INTRODUCTION

I don't remember exactly when, but sometime in 1969 I made a decision to trade a perfectly fine Pontiac Catalina convertible for a sensational-looking new car. It was love at first sight. I absolutely, positively had to have it, now! Forget the cost. Forget logic. My emotions and my stupid male ego were out of control, running rampant in the direction of my local Buick dealer. There, on the showroom floor, stood "my" forest green Opel GT, imported from Germany and looking every bit like the Ferrari or Corvette its designers had shamelessly copied.

What followed probably served me right for being so impulsive. From day one, the Opel GT gave me mechanical fits. Its engine ran rough at all speeds. What was worse, the thing would quit cold while I was going 65 miles per hour in the left lane on the expressway. With some perseverance it would restart, only to quit again a few more miles down the road.

How many times was I forced to nurse that rotten bucket of bolts back to the dealership? How many times were my pleadings to the service manager repeated? How many times was his promise of satisfaction played back? Too many times, but what was I to do? The dealer hadn't a clue as to how the problem could be repaired.

Finally, after more than six months, and with my patience long since exhausted, an ultimatum was delivered to the dealer via my

> *Had I known then what I know now about automobile Lemon Laws, my problems would have been solved sooner*

attorney: "Find the problem and fix it or face a law suit." You never saw such a flurry of activity. Mechanics and engineers from Buick Motor Division conducted an inspection with thoroughness normally reserved for commercial airliners and rides at Disney World. We're talking about the whole nine yards - from X-rays to diagnostic computers to stripping and rebuilding the engine, part by part.

And then, there it was. So obvious that no one had noticed. So simple that no one could imagine it as the cause of such egregious problems. With one bolt and a couple of twists on a socket wrench...my ordeal was over. The grounding cable from the engine block was re-attached to the chassis and the engine went hummmmmmmmmmm.

The next day I went to the nearest Chevy dealer and bought a new car.

Had I known then what I know now about automobile Lemon Laws, my problems would have been solved sooner. Unfortunately, in 1969 there weren't any Lemon Laws. They only became a part of our legal system after Congress passed the Magnuson-Moss Warranty Act in 1975. In fact, the first state Lemon Law was not passed until 1982. Today, however, almost all states have enacted Lemon Law legislation which provides consumers with a clearly defined set of rights and recourse should repetitive problems occur within the first 12 to 24 months of automobile ownership.

"Lemon Aid" was created to provide you with the most valuable tool available to a new car owner: KNOWLEDGE. Whether or not you're currently experiencing a recurring problem with your car, this book will benefit you. You'll acquire knowledge to protect yourself and your financial interests, the knowledge of how to complain and to whom to direct a complaint, and knowledge of what your rights are as a consumer and how to exercise those rights.

"Lemon Aid" provides the basic information you'll need to assess the scope and nature of your problem, decide if it qualifies for due process under your state's Lemon Law, evaluate your procedural options and decide how to act. The book's appendices provide the necessary information to take immediate action.

"Lemon Aid" can help you exercise your rights and regain your rightful position in the driver's seat!

1
THE CHANGING RELATIONSHIP BETWEEN AUTOMOTIVE MANUFACTURERS AND CONSUMERS

Owning a new car or truck should be a pleasurable experience. Whether your decision to buy a car was to meet basic transportation needs or to fulfill your life-long dream of owning the ultimate luxury or sports car, you don't *expect* to experience problems.

There is no argument that today's cars far surpass those of yesterday in every category. But, today's car, unlike the horseless carriage of 100 years ago or even this author's Opel GT of 20 years ago, is a sophisticated, highly complex system of mechanical and electronic parts assembled by humans and robots. Things can and do go wrong.

Chances are good you did a good deal of research before deciding on which car to buy. You may have read everything from *Road and Track* to *Consumer Reports*, researching which makes and models would best meet your needs. You probably talked with friends about their experiences with local dealers and with various auto manufacturers. By the time you purchased your car, you had likely developed certain expectations...about the car, the dealer and the manufacturer. So, what happens when those expectations are not met?

The relationship between the automotive industry and the American consumer is undergoing dramatic and unprecedented change

> *The collective voice of the consumer has become a force powerful enough to convince federal and state officials that the time has arrived for automotive consumer legislation.*

largely as a result of increasing competition and more active consumerism. Understanding these changes and their effects will aid you in resolving problems with your automobile.

CHANGES IN COMPETITION

Three primary forces have contributed to the increasing competition in the automotive market. They are:

- Geo-political Events
- Technological Parity
- Increased Production Capacity

Geo-political Events

Not until the oil crisis of the 1970s did competition from imports challenge the mass market dominance of domestic auto makers. The politics of energy crystallized the need for efficient use of finite natural resources and gave import manufacturers their entree into mass-market America. More and more Americans purchased imported cars. They were more fuel-efficient than domestic cars, of at least comparable quality and dollar for dollar were perceived as a better value. Imports were fast becoming an acceptable alternative to domestic vehicles in the minds of middle America and the gas-guzzler headed towards history's parking lot. The scaled-down, energy conservative vehicle became a symbol of a more energy - and value - conscious America.

Imports increased their market share in the United States from 18% in 1978 to 31% in 1988, according to *Automotive News,* an industry journal. Domestic manufacturers have responded to this market presence by offering a product line that more closely matches the needs and desires of customers and reflects an increasing emphasis on product quality.

Technological Parity

Advances in automotive technology bring state-of-the-art sophistication to today's consumers. The evolution of technology has allowed manufacturers to incorporate new and innovative features into their product line. Yet, the technological distinction between vehicles has narrowed to the point where it is difficult to distinguish one vehicle or manufacturer from another. In recent years, the sharing of technological innovation within the automotive industry has produced comparable vehicles within each class, thereby intensifying competition.

Increased Production Capacity

Asian and European manufacturers have expanded their production capacity by establishing U. S. manufacturing facilities. In addition, many domestic manufacturers now supplement their existing product line by purchasing vehicles manufactured outside of the United States.

Thus, the current production of vehicles has reversed the historic over-demand/under-supply tradition in the industry. In fact, it is estimated that in 1990 there are 15 million vehicles in the U.S. for only 11 million buyers. It is unlikely, therefore, that the ferocity of competition among auto makers witnessed in the last few years will abate.

CONSUMERISM

It is not just competition that is the driving force behind the industry's very keen interest in customer satisfaction, but a consumer consciousness that has been gaining momentum since the 1960s. Personalities like Ralph Nader and David Horowitz are synonymous with consumer activism. Consumer advocacy groups have gained momentum and continue to spearhead the drive to educate and inform consumers. The collective voice of the consumer has become a force powerful enough to convince federal and state officials that the time has arrived for automotive consumer legislation.

IMPACT ON CONSUMERS

With relatively comparable vehicles in abundant supply, how are manufacturers to distinguish their product? Today, they rely heavily upon their ability to create a perception of being "customer-friendly." That is, having people and policies behind their products which create favorable consumer feelings and, thereby, influence consumer purchase decisions. Customer satisfaction - the ability to consistently meet customer expectations and retain loyalty - is the key to success in the marketplace of the 1990s.

The good news for consumers is that automotive manufacturers are increasingly aware of this trend. A great deal of effort is being directed toward quantifying customer satisfaction. The introduction of publicized surveys and rankings of customer attitudes has irrevocably altered the industry's views about and commitment to customer satisfaction. The combination of increased manufacturer and dealer responsiveness to consumers and strong, pro-consumer legislation creates an environment where the consumer can obtain satisfaction more easily than ever before.

2

THE CASE OF JOHN T. CONSUMER

In order to help you understand how Lemon Laws work and how to exercise your rights under the laws, throughout the chapters of "Lemon Aid" we'll refer to the fictitious, but all-too-familiar experiences of John T. Consumer, an average guy who finds himself with new car problems that won't go away. Any similarity between Mr. Consumer and persons sharing Mr. Consumer's frustrations is not the least bit coincidental.

June 15th - Odometer reading: 3 miles

Mr. Consumer takes delivery of a beautiful, new automobile from the dealer on 5th and Main. He slips behind the wheel, fastens his seat belt, adjusts the power seat and mirrors, then reaches for the ignition. Instantly, the car's 3.5 liter, turbo-charged, 240 horsepower, twin-cam, 24 valve, computer-controlled, fuel injected engine comes to life.

Mr. Consumer - we'll call him John - is now in command, seated in the ergonomic driver's compartment. He surveys the space-age, digital instrumentation designed to monitor the pulse of the car's computer-controlled systems. He smiles. His brand new machine, one and a half tons of sculpted metal in motion, promises to deliver high-performance, fuel efficiency and trouble-free operation. What more could he ask for?

July 6th - Odometer reading: 773 miles

John returns to the dealership, complaining of a strange noise and roughness in the engine's operation. The dealer's service manager assures John it's not a problem; the noise will disappear and the engine will smooth-out after the break-in period. Nevertheless, John asks the service manager to write-up his complaint and asks to have a mechanic check out the problems. About two hours later the report comes back that nothing appears to be wrong. John accepts the service manager's advice that his concerns will soon disappear. He leaves the dealership with renewed confidence in his new car.

October 10th - Odometer reading: 4,023 miles

John returns to the dealer. He's obviously distressed that the engine noise is still present and the roughness seems to be getting worse. Once again, he presents his problem to the dealer's service manager and requests an inspection. The service order is written-up and John is told to return after 4:30 pm that day.

John returns to the dealership after work to claim his car. The service manager advises him that the noise is a normal operating characteristic of his car, and that the roughness was minimized by a few minor adjustments. John leaves the dealership and, within a few minutes, realizes that the roughness is still very evident. A feeling of anger and frustration comes over John. His disappointment and dissatisfaction over both the car's performance and the dealer's response is growing.

October 24th - Odometer reading: 4,570 miles

Two weeks after his second visit to the dealer, John is driving home from work when the engine noise suddenly gets louder. Then, without any warning, the engine quits at a traffic light. John finds a nearby phone, calls the dealer and demands a tow truck. An hour and twenty minutes later, John climbs into the cab of the tow truck and begins rehearsing exactly what he'll say to the dealer. He promises himself he'll be business-like and will control his temper. But, he assures himself that he'll settle for no less than complete satisfaction.

The dealer proves very sympathetic to John's plight and assures him that his car will be restored to a like-new condition. When John requests a loaner, however, the dealer tells him there is no loaner policy and advises of a conveniently-located car rental agency down the street. Four hours after his ordeal began, John pulls in his driveway. Exasperated, he heads right for his desk drawer, pulls out the warranty on his new car, and begins to read...

3
AUTOMOBILE WARRANTIES AND THE HISTORY OF LEMON LAW LEGISLATION

What does a warranty mean? Americans expect a warranty to protect them from a product that does not perform up to the standards promoted by the manufacturer. With small ticket items, the warranty usually means a defective product will be replaced by the distributor or manufacturer, or the purchase price refunded. Generally, the more expensive a product the less likely it is that warranty coverage provides for a refund or replacement. Previously, the interpretation of an automotive warranty meant repairs would be done at no charge ... as many times as necessary. A refund or replacement of a car was uncommon in the automotive industry.

The enactment of the Lemon Laws has significantly impacted the interpretation of a vehicle warranty by limiting the number of unsuccessful repair attempts before requiring the manufacturer to offer a refund or replacement of the vehicle. This chapter provides a brief history of the creation of Lemon Law legislation.

Magnuson-Moss Warranty Act

The origin of Lemon Law dates back to 1975 when Congress passed the Magnuson-Moss Warranty Act. Its primary purpose was to define written warranties on consumer products ranging from typewrit-

> **Lemon Law reflects the spirit of the Magnuson-Moss Warranty Act but applies specifically to automobiles**

ers to automobiles. It established the party responsible for upholding the warranty to be the writer of the warranty, not the supplier or distributor of the product. Thus, the legislation firmly identified that the automobile manufacturer, not the dealer, is primarily responsible for upholding the terms of the warranty. A key provision of the Act further encouraged manufacturers to establish an informal dispute settlement procedure or arbitration program for customers to use in resolving warranty complaints. Technically, these programs differ from arbitration in that they are not binding upon the consumer. Nevertheless, "Lemon Aid" uses the term 'arbitration' to describe the process since the industry commonly describes their programs this way.

FTC Rule 703

Following passage of the Magnuson-Moss Warranty Act, the Federal Trade Commission (FTC) set forth regulations to implement the provisions of the Act regarding informal dispute resolution procedures. FTC's Rule 703 details the duties of the warrantor (writer of the warranty) and identifies minimum requirements for an arbitration program.

The manufacturer is required under Rule 703 to advise consumers of the availability of arbitration at the time of purchase. The Rule further specifies operational requirements for the arbitration program, qualifications of the arbitrators, time frames for resolution, record-keeping and audit requirements, and requires that the arbitration be provided at no charge to the consumer.

The intent of the legislation was to provide consumers the full benefit of a manufacturer's warranty and be able to resolve a dispute concerning warranty performance outside of the court system. These important first steps toward consumer-oriented legislation set the stage for Lemon Laws.

State Lemon Laws

Automobile manufacturers did not initially respond as hoped to this federal legislation which encouraged establishment of arbitration programs. The FTC's monitoring role proved ineffective and little actually changed with regard to dispute resolution in the auto industry.

With growing emphasis on consumerism and the minimal effect of this federal legislation, the states began to look at strengthening consumer protection through stricter statutes regulating the automotive industry. Recognizing that the purchase of an automobile was a major economic investment for the consumer, second only to the purchase of a home, states began to consider enactment of legislation to offer consumer redress if a manufacturer was unable to conform an automobile to its warranty after a reasonable number of repair attempts.

Connecticut, in 1982, was the first state to pass legislation requiring automotive manufacturers to refund the consumer's purchase price or replace the automobile if a problem was not resolved in a reasonable manner. Rapidly, other states followed suit. As of April, 1990, such laws have been enacted in 48 states and the District of Columbia. These refund/replace laws have become commonly known as Lemon Laws.

The laws reflect the spirit of the Magnuson-Moss Act but apply specifically to motor vehicles. They specify that the manufacturer can no longer meet its warranty obligations through repeated repairs. If warrantable repairs are not successful in a specified number of attempts or within a reasonable period of time, the consumer is entitled to a refund or replacement.

Second and Third Generation Lemon Laws

Many states have re-evaluated and modified their statutes with the knowledge gained from administering the first generation of Lemon Laws. These second and even third generation Lemon Laws reflect increased support from constituents for this legislation. By and large, the changes afford the consumer more protection by extending coverage, clarifying and expanding awards, reducing the number of repair attempts and creating state-run arbitration boards.

While Lemon Laws are still evolving, one thing is certain: they have shifted the balance of power from manufacturers to consumers and are impacting the ways in which the automobile industry does business.

4

A DEFINITION AND EXPLANATION OF LEMON LAW LEGISLATION

**October 25th - Odometer reading: 4,579 miles
(The odometer rolled-up 9 miles in tow to the dealer)**

It's the day after John Consumer's new car was brought into the dealership "on the hook." John receives a call from the dealer's Service Manager, who advises that his car needs a short block replacement.

"It seems like a bigger problem than it actually is," says the Service Manager. "Every so often we've got to replace a short block that passes all the factory inspections but develops problems once the car's on the road. The replacement part's been ordered. It should be here in about three days and take two days to install. Your car will be as good as new in a week. I've also called the Zone Office Rep to see if they'll pick up the cost of your rental car."

Over a cup of coffee later that morning, John explains his plight and frustrations to a fellow worker. "The car's brand new and I'm having half the engine replaced. The way things are going," moans John, "I think I got one of those lemons."

John's friend's eyes light-up. "Hey! In last Sunday's paper I read about a book that some guy wrote on the automobile Lemon Laws. I think it was called "Lemon Aid." It's supposed to tell you what your rights are and who to contact for help. You ought to get the book and find out what the Lemon Laws are all about."

* * * *

As indicated in **Chapter 3**, Lemon Law is the term commonly used to identify state laws which offer a refund or replacement vehicle to a consumer who owns an automobile with an uncorrected, substantial problem. The California Department of Consumer Affairs describes the law as follows:

> *The law creates what is known in legal terminology as a presumption; the Lemon Law presumes that you are entitled to a refund or a replacement if the manufacturer or its dealer has made a certain number of unsuccessful attempts to repair your car.*

The manufacturer's written warranty guarantees repairs for a defect in material or workmanship under normal use within the stated time and mileage limitations. Warranty coverage allows an unlimited number of repair opportunities with no recourse if those repairs are not successful. **The Lemon Law restricts repair attempts to a reasonable number on the same defect and requires the manufacturer to either replace the vehicle or refund the purchase price if the problem is not corrected and substantially impairs the vehicle's use, value or safety. It also limits the number of days a vehicle can be out of service within a specified period due to repairs before the manufacturer is required to either replace the vehicle or refund its purchase price.**

UNDERSTANDING LEMON LAW TERMS

Many terms used routinely in Lemon Laws are unfamiliar to average consumers. The following definitions will help clarify Lemon Law terminology:

Express Limited Warranty

The written warranty provided by the manufacturer at the time of purchase. This does not include any extended warranty, offered independently by a dealership or other entity, purchased by a consumer.

Implied Warranty

The manufacturer's assurance that the vehicle is fit for its intended use and meets reasonable expectations for its performance.

Nonconformity

A problem which causes the vehicle to fail to meet the standards created by either the express or implied warranty.

Informal Dispute Settlement Mechanism

An independent, third-party mediation program provided by the manufacturer. Although commonly referred to as arbitration, the results of such a procedure are not binding on the consumer. The consumer can, if dissatisfied, pursue the matter through other channels such as the court system.

Some Lemon Laws require the consumer to first utilize the manufacturer's informal dispute settlement mechanism if the program has been reviewed by the state and meets certain criteria. This review is commonly termed certification.

Repair Attempt

An effort undertaken by the manufacturer or an authorized dealer to correct a problem which constitutes a nonconformity. Repairs by independent repair shops do not qualify under the Lemon Laws. A written repair order must be available to document the repair attempt. Repairs should not be confused with normal vehicle maintenance such as an oil change.

FTC

The Federal Trade Commission, a governmental body authorized to regulate business practices to ensure fair trade.

Rule 703

Guidelines established by the FTC to implement provisions of Magnuson-Moss Act regarding informal dispute settlement procedures.

Definition and Explanation 15

Magnuson-Moss Act

Federal legislation encouraging manufacturers to uphold terms of consumer product warranties.

UNDERSTANDING LEMON LAW PROVISIONS

Although existing Lemon Laws vary by state, they do contain common provisions. **Appendix I** includes a summary of the provisions of each state's Lemon Law. The major provisions common to Lemon Laws are explained below.

■ Qualifying Vehicles

Which vehicles are eligible? Normally, coverage is limited to new vehicles purchased and/or registered within a state, or situations when the vehicle is transferred from one individual to another during the express warranty period.

Most states limit coverage to vehicles used primarily for personal use and exclude commercial vehicles. A commercial vehicle is usually defined as one used primarily for business purposes or registered to a business entity. Also detailed in the legislation are specific exclusions to coverage which typically include vehicles such as motorcycles, off-road vehicles, or motor homes.

Few states included leased vehicles in their original Lemon Law coverage. However, as laws are being revised, many states are including coverage for leased vehicles.

■ Length of Coverage

How long is a car covered? The length of coverage is defined by the period of time from original delivery or by the number of miles on the vehicle's odometer or the manufacturer's express warranty period. Coverage is generally the earlier of a time or mileage limitation or the earlier of a time or warranty limitation. Each state has established different limitations.

■ Qualifying Non-Conformity

What car problems are eligible? The problem with the car must substantially impair the vehicle's:

- Use; or
- Value; or
- Safety

The problem with the car must not result from:

- Improper maintenance (negligence);
- Improper use (abuse);
- Changes by the owner (modifications);
- Accidents

In other words, a manufacturer can successfully defend a Lemon Law case if the reported nonconformity was caused by the consumer's action and not a result of deficiencies in the manufactured quality of the vehicle.

■ Required Number of Repairs or Out of Service Days

How many repairs/service days qualify? The laws specify how many unsuccessful repair attempts are allowed by either the dealer or manufacturer for the same problem. Some also specify an overall number of allowable repairs for differing problems.

The laws also specify how many total days are allowed for a car to be out of service for repair attempts.

■ Eligibility

How does a vehicle become eligible? Eligibility is defined as meeting either the criteria for number of repair attempts or the number of days out of service.

■ Consumer Procedures

What does the consumer have to do? Most states require the consumer to notify the manufacturer in writing of the problem. In many states, the consumer must allow the manufacturer one additional opportunity to correct the problem. If the problem remains unresolved, the consumer may initiate a formal action against the manufacturer according to the process described in the consumer's state Lemon Law.

■ Manufacturer's Informal Dispute Settlement Mechanism

What's the next step after written notification? Some states specify the consumer must first use an informal dispute settlement mechanism (arbitration program) if the manufacturer has established one and if it substantially complies with FTC Rule 703. In addition, some states with this requirement further specify that it only applies if the state has certified the manufacturer's dispute settlement mechanism program. More details are available in **Chapter 8**.

■ Awards

What does the consumer receive? The overall intent of the Lemon Laws is to provide the consumer with a comparable replacement vehicle or a refund of the purchase price.

Most states deduct a reasonable amount for the consumer's use of the vehicle and for any damage not attributed to normal wear and tear. However, other items which may be included in calculating the amount due the consumer in addition to the purchase price are:

- Registration/sales tax
- Governmental charges
- Other collateral charges
- Options installed by dealer
- Finance charges
- Towing/rental car expenses
  incurred as a result of the problem

■ Mileage Deduction

Is there a deduction for mileage driven? Generally, yes. The deduction for consumer use is based on either the amount of miles at the first report of the nonconformity or the amount of miles at the time of repurchase. The guidelines in **Appendix I** detail the provisions for each state.

The amount deducted for mileage is determined either by computing a certain monetary amount per mile driven, or by using a formula based on the purchase price of the vehicle multiplied by a fraction created with the mileage as the numerator and 100,000 (or the figure prescribed by your state's Lemon Law) as the denominator. Example: $25,000 x 5,000/100,000.

Regardless of the method used by the state, the intent is to fairly deduct for the use the consumer received from the vehicle.

■ Leased Vehicles

Are leased vehicles covered under Lemon Laws? In some states, yes. Compensation for a leased vehicle is generally the same as for purchased vehicles. Details are outlined in the state summaries, included in **Appendix I**.

5
DOCUMENTING YOUR CAR'S HISTORY AND HOW TO PROPERLY ADVISE YOUR DEALER OF NEEDED REPAIRS

November 2nd - Odometer reading: 4,799 miles

The phone rings and John answers. It's the dealership calling to advise that the short block has been replaced and the car is ready. That afternoon, John drives out of the dealership feeling confident his problems are over. After all, his car practically has a brand new engine. John rationalizes all his aggravation and lost time by telling himself that a new short block should prolong the life of his car. What could be better?

John smiles as he recalls how angry he was with the dealer and the car. *Lemon? Forget it!* thinks John. *This car and I are going to spend some quality time together in the years ahead.* Nevertheless, he tucks away in the back of his mind the information on the Lemon Laws he gained from reading that little book called "Lemon Aid."

November 30th - Odometer reading: 5,679 miles

John pulls into his local service station to fill 'er up and is a bit surprised when he notices that his oil is almost two quarts low. He drives another 500 miles then again checks his oil.

"A quart low? What the hell's going on?," John mumbles aloud. He's seen no evidence of an oil leak in his garage.

As he reaches for the telephone to once again call the dealer, that ominous feeling comes over John. His stomach begins churning. The Service Manager, sounding a bit frustrated, willingly schedules an immediate appointment. Meanwhile, John becomes acutely aware of the fact that the engine is suddenly making "that" noise again.

While driving to the dealership, John reviews in his mind the Lemon Law provisions he read. He makes a mental note that this will be his fourth visit for repair of the same problem, and to ensure that his repair order is properly documented...just in case.

* * * *

Being a smart consumer does take effort. Reviewing bills and keeping receipts are personal record-keeping responsibilities which can be tedious and often are left undone. **Complete record-keeping is strongly recommended whether or not you experience a problem.** If you should experience a recurring problem, your records can assist you in making a strong and convincing presentation in the event Lemon Law action becomes necessary. This chapter instructs you on responsible record-keeping and notification requirements which must be fulfilled in order to protect your rights.

Required Maintenance Records

A motor vehicle, no matter what make or model, requires ongoing maintenance to assure its continued performance. In your owner's manual, the manufacturer details the basic maintenance requirements which

> *Records management must begin the day the vehicle is driven from the showroom.*

must be fulfilled in order to receive warranty benefits. Since many problems with a car can be directly attributed to the lack of required maintenance, manufacturers will request maintenance records when considering some warranty claims.

A common question among car owners is whether independent maintenance or do-it-yourself maintenance voids the new car warranty. Manufacturers can (and do) ask to see maintenance records. Although their preference is that the vehicle maintenance is performed by an authorized dealership, the requirement is only that the maintenance is performed and documented.

Consumers should keep a detailed record of all servicing done to a vehicle. The record should include:
- Date
- Odometer reading
- Vehicle identification number
- Clear statement of work performed

In the case of dealer servicing, the written service order is your proof that proper and necessary maintenance procedures were performed. Consumers who perform their own maintenance should keep similar records and it might not be a bad idea to have someone witness your documentation.

Records management must begin the day the vehicle is driven from the showroom. Copies of work records and dealer work orders should be kept in a safe location other than in your car's glove compartment.

It is also essential to obtain and keep all service records for unscheduled repair work. Request a work order for every repair. Which means, even if you drive out, reach the corner, determine that the problem persists, and drive back to the dealer...get a new repair order written-up. Do not allow the dealer to do any work on the old order. Each new order signifies another attempt at repair. Remember from **Chapter 4** that the number of repair attempts and/or the number of days a car is out of service are important considerations in any Lemon Law action.

How To Report Problems To The Dealer

When you take your car to a dealership for servicing, ***even under warranty***, it's important to be sure you properly report any problems so the dealer can accurately write them up. This section presents some basic guidelines to follow.

First, insure the work order contains the basics:

- date
- odometer reading
- vehicle identification number
- a clear statement of work performed

Only then should you sign the work order. If the car is not ready the same day, the dates on the work order should accurately reflect the number of days out of service. If not, have them entered before you accept the car and leave the dealership.

Secondly, since the work order is written by a dealer representative, inspect the written description of the problem (nonconformity). Is it accurate? Does it clearly identify the problems *as you've stated them?* It is your responsibility to protect your interests by verifying the information on the work order. If you have trouble expressing yourself, by all means write-out a description before you go the dealer. Make a duplicate of your note and request that the dealer attach a copy to his part of the work order as well as yours.

Lastly, if you are returning for the same problem, ensure that the terminology used on the work order to describe the problem is similar to what was written on previous orders. Many Lemon Laws rely upon work orders to verify that it was, in fact, the same nonconformity which was reported and that a reasonable number of repair attempts were performed on that nonconformity. *If the description of the problem isn't similar, your case could be at risk.*

In order to insure continuity from one work order to the next, you may want to ask the service writer to reference the previous work order numbers on the current one. Not only will this strengthen your documentation but it will also alert dealer personnel that this is a repeat repair. This may initiate more concentrated efforts by the dealer to resolve your problem.

Again, it's important to file copies of work orders in a safe place, away from your car.

6

RESOLVING YOUR COMPLAINT WITH THE DEALER OR MANUFACTURER BEFORE TAKING LEMON LAW ACTION

December 1st - Odometer reading: 5,688 miles

While John's car is in for another round of service, he rechecks his copy of "Lemon Aid" and decides that if things aren't fixed this time, he's going direct to the manufacturer with his complaint.

The next afternoon, John picks up his car and heads for home. His ears are tuned to the slightest noise. All seems well and the days roll by without incident...

December 16th - Odometer reading: 6,108 miles

"I can't believe it!" says John to the service station attendant. "The oil's how many quarts low? That can't be. The car's been out of the shop less than three weeks and I've put less than 400 miles on it. I'm burning a quart of oil every 200 miles."

John's beside himself and he begins agonizing over what's coming next. Another trip to the dealer. More inconvenience. More disappointment? He slams his hand on the car hood.

"That's it!" he shouts. "I'm not going to put up with this garbage. It's time to play hardball."

John's attempts to have the problem resolved through the dealer have been fruitless. To make matters worse, he's lost confidence in the dealer. Therefore, John decides it's time to take his case directly to the manufacturer.

* * * *

Perhaps one of the most difficult judgments to make after you've exhausted your patience with the dealer is whether to initiate action under the Lemon Laws or bring additional pressure to bear on the dealer and manufacturer to resolve your problem.

Generally, it is more effective to attempt resolution, at least initially, through the dealer or the manufacturer. The information provided in this chapter is designed to give you some "how-tos" on confronting the dealer and/or the manufacturer.

There are two main types of complaints:
- **Dealership complaints** - which relate to sales issues or quality of dealer service.
- **Manufacturer complaints** - which relate to product quality, performance or warranty coverage.

Dealership Complaints

Sales transactions relate to the cost of a vehicle, its financing or unfulfilled promises made by dealer personnel. Complaints of this nature are between the customer and the dealership. The dealership is generally a franchise business and regulatory laws limit manufacturer intervention in sales transactions.

In disputes of this nature, where you are unable to obtain satisfaction directly from the dealer, you may still wish to contact the manufacturer. Although technically unable to take direct action, the manufacturer may be able to aid in resolving your complaint. If unsuccessful, you might consider taking the matter to your local Better Business Bureau or the Consumer Rights or Consumer Protection Division of your state's Attorney General. See State Contact Information in **Appendix I.**

Service complaints are less clearly defined. It is often difficult for the consumer to determine whether the fault lies with the dealership or the manufacturer. For example, an unresolved defect may stem from improper dealer repairs or a manufacturing design or product defect. When the responsible party is not clearly defined and the dealer has not resolved the situation, it is best to involve the manufacturer.

Dealership Complaint Resolution

As stated earlier, automobile dealerships are independent businesses that purchase a vehicle from a manufacturer and subsequently sell it to the consumer. The dealership, particularly in today's competitive market, values the individual customer and relies heavily on word-of-mouth advertising. Situated at the "front line," the dealership is the first place to attempt resolution of a problem.

Generally, dealerships are divided into three areas of operation - Sales, Service and Parts. The nature of your complaint will determine which department is the most appropriate to approach.

If you are unable to resolve the problem with the initial contact person, the department's manager is your next step. For example, if the service writer does not resolve your problem, ask to see the Service Manager.

If this is unsuccessful, some dealerships have designated a customer relations or public relations manager as another appeal level. Failing to resolve your situation at this level, the general manager or owner may represent the final step in the resolution process at the dealer level.

Remember, when you are dealing with dealership personnel, first and foremost you are their customer. Each customer can bring additional profit to the dealership through service, future purchases, and personal referral. Remind the dealership that you are a potential future customer for sales and service and wish to resolve the situation satisfactorily to the benefit of both parties. A satisfied customer is a victory for everyone.

Manufacturer Complaints

A complaint against a manufacturer results primarily from a product defect or warranty coverage denial. These types of problems are beyond the dealership's control and responsibility for their resolution rests with the manufacturer.

When you contact an automotive manufacturer, be prepared to provide information on the vehicle, service history, current problem and requested assistance. This will enable the manufacturer to evaluate and appropriately respond to your particular problem.

Other points to remember include:

- Try to make most of your contacts <u>in writing.</u>
- If you call or visit, record the following information immediately after your contact:
    - Time
    - Date
    - Summary of conversation
    - Name of individual to whom you spoke
- Retain copies of everything sent to the manufacturer.
- Never provide original work orders (you may need them if the situation escalates to arbitration or court action).

As with work orders, the documentation you keep is critical to the successful presentation of your case under the Lemon Law.

Manufacturer Complaint Resolution

Your problem may be brought to the attention of the manufacturer in two ways. The dealership may make contact with the manufacturer on your behalf or you may elect to contact the manufacturer directly.

• Dealer Communication with Manufacturer

It is common for a dealership to contact their manufacturer to request assistance on behalf of their customers. Using your dealer as a mediator between you and the manufacturer may be the most expeditious and effective means of complaint resolution. In fact, many dealers are aggressive in requesting a review of a customer's complaint by the manufacturer.

• Consumer Communication with Manufacturer

Since manufacturers are as interested in satisfying customers as their dealers, they have established direct channels for consumers to use in resolving problems. More than half of the manufacturers now maintain toll-free numbers for customer convenience. Other manufacturers resolve customer problems either through their zone or regional offices or corporate customer relations departments.

If you are unsure about whether to contact a zone or regional office or the corporate headquarters, read through your owner's manual or consult your dealer. If you have already contacted a zone or regional office and remain dissatisfied, you may wish to contact the company's corporate headquarters. However, in most cases the corporate office delegates customer handling and complaint resolution to the appropriate zone or regional office. Contact information for most manufacturers is included in **Appendix II** of this book for your convenience.

A final thought: If you have been unsuccessful in obtaining a satisfactory repair through your dealer and are reasonably certain your situation qualifies for Lemon Law action, you may want to initiate Lemon Law action at the same time you contact the manufacturer. In most states, Lemon Law stipulates that a manufacturer will be entitled to one final attempt at repair before arbitration proceedings begin. So, why not make the manufacturer's attempt at repair part of the formal process and save some time.

Under any circumstances, the process to initiate formal Lemon Law action begins with a **Demand Letter** to the manufacturer. This letter and the entire process will be covered in the next two chapters.

7

INITIATING ACTION UNDER THE LEMON LAWS

January 10th - Odometer reading: 6,550 miles

John turns to the manufacturer for help and his effort produces an almost immediate response. Everyone from the manufacturer's zone office is extremely cooperative. John is again given use of rental car at no cost while the manufacturer's service supervisors and dealer mechanics wrestle with the problem. Within a week, John and his car are together again, this time with assurances that the problem has been diagnosed and properly repaired.

February 6th - Odometer reading: 7,445 miles

It's a bright, but chilly February morning and John is on his way to work. Suddenly, without warning, the dashboard lights all come on, the car quickly loses power, and John coasts to the shoulder of the road. Gripping the steering wheel so tightly his knuckles turn white, John shouts to himself, "Not again! Why me?"

The tow truck driver remembers John from last October. He chuckles, "Quite a lemon you've got there, buddy." John fumes.

Later that day, the dealer's Service Manager calls. "I'm afraid it's going to need another short block. I know you're not the least bit happy, but we'll do our best to make sure this is the final repair. And by the way," he adds, "the Zone Rep says he'll cover your rental car cost."

John slams the telephone receiver onto its cradle. "That's it! I've had enough. No more getting angry. It's time to get satisfaction."

* * * *

Lemon Law Notification

Most states require that you initiate the Lemon Law process with a formal notification to the manufacturer that you intend to seek protection under the Lemon Law. Notification such as this is known as a **Demand Letter** since you are demanding that the manufacturer repair the vehicle or you will pursue Lemon Law action. A sample of such a demand letter can be found in this chapter (**Figure 1**). Although not specifically required in every state, it is advisable to send such notification by certified mail, return receipt requested.

Your Demand Letter will usually result in the manufacturer having one final attempt to affect repairs to your satisfaction. However, the manufacturer is not obligated to make the attempt if it does not believe the work is justified. In the event suitable repairs are not made, or if the manufacturer refuses to make the attempt, formal proceedings under the Lemon Law can begin.

WORKING YOUR WAY THROUGH A COMPLAINT

There is a very specific process which both you and the manufacturer will follow in reaching a conclusion on your Lemon Law complaint. Although the process may vary by state, a generalized summary follows in the next chapter for each of the three courses of action you may elect to use. These summaries are intended to familiarize you with the processes so you'll better understand what is involved in reaching a final resolution.

The three avenues of resolution are:

- **Manufacturer's Informal Dispute Settlement Mechanism**
- **State Arbitration**
- **Civil Court**

It is important to note these three avenues are not mutually exclusive unless specified by the state. For example, a consumer who is dissatisfied with the decision under manufacturer's informal dispute settlement may pursue action through state arbitration or in civil court. Additionally, in most states the consumer retains all other existing rights

SAMPLE DEMAND LETTER (MANUFACTURER NOTIFICATION)

(Date)

Dear (Manufacturer):

My car qualifies for refund or replacement for the nonconformity described below under the lemon law in (State). This letter is written notification of the problem as required by law and represents my demand for relief. Pertinent information is as follows:

YEAR/MODEL_____

VEHICLE IDENTIFICATION NUMBER_____

DATE OF PURCHASE_____

MILEAGE_____

SERVICING DEALER_____

NONCONFORMITY_____

Outlined below are details regarding previous repair attempts:

DATE   DEALER   MILEAGE   DESCRIPTION

1._____

2._____

3._____

4._____

As you can see by the repair history, the statutory requirements for relief have been met.

Please be advised that I will pursue relief under the lemon law if this nonconformity is not immediately repaired.

Sincerely,

Figure 1- Demand Letter

and remedies under law. In some states, the consumer may choose whether to first use the manufacturer's or the state's arbitration program. In other states, the course of action is defined by statute.

Manufacturer's Informal Dispute Settlement Mechanism (Manufacturer's Arbitration)

Many manufacturers now offer an independent, third-party informal dispute settlement mechanism to resolve disputes. Since most manufacturers refer to this mechanism as arbitration, we will use the terms interchangeably. Provisions of manufacturer's arbitration include:

- No cost to consumer;
- Cases resolved on a timely basis;
- Manufacturer agrees to accept decision as binding;
- Coverage may extend beyond the time/mileage limitations specified in the Lemon Law;
- Legal counsel not required;
- Awards not limited to repair/replace, but may include reimbursement for repairs, additional repairs at no charge, or other similar compromises.

A manufacturer's arbitration program is easily accessed by the consumer. Often, information about arbitration availability is provided in the vehicle owner's manual, at the dealership, or in a statement provided at the time of purchase. **Appendix III** includes information on manufacturer's arbitration programs.

A consumer who wishes to initiate arbitration through the manufacturer should contact the appropriate zone, regional or corporate office as specified in the owner's manual and request necessary information. Most manufacturers will provide an application to be completed and returned to the arbitration agency.

State laws may require the consumer to first use the manufacturer's arbitration program under one or both of the following conditions:

- The arbitration program substantially complies with FTC Rule 703.
- The state has certified the manufacturer's arbitration mechanism.

This means the consumer cannot initiate state arbitration or civil court action until they first utilize the manufacturer's arbitration program. Otherwise, there is a risk of losing some relief provided under Magnuson-Moss. This requirement is known as **prior resort.**

However, the consumer can initiate state arbitration or civil court action after pursuing manufacturer's arbitration if dissatisfied with the decision. Also, if the consumer is seeking compensation outside the scope and provisions of the Lemon Law — such as punitive damages (a payment made as punishment for an offense), monetary compensation for personal injury, property damages or lost wages — a civil court action is required. Lemon Law arbitration programs apply only to resolution of disputes through refund or replacement of the vehicle.

State Arbitration

Some states have included as part of their Lemon Law a state-administered arbitration board. As with the Manufacturer's Informal Dispute Settlement Mechanism, these programs are commonly known as arbitration although they are not binding upon the consumer. For simplicity, we will refer to them as arbitration boards. Provisions of state arbitration include:

- An application fee in some states;
- Cases resolved on a timely basis;
- Coverage limited to Lemon Law eligibility;
- Legal counsel not required;
- Awards limited to refund/replace;
- Decision binding on manufacturer but not consumer.

Information about the availability of state arbitration boards is available through your state's Office of the Attorney General or Consumer Protection Agency. **Appendix III** also includes contact information for state arbitration boards. A consumer who wishes to utilize a state-administered arbitration board must contact the appropriate state office to request the application forms. As with all manufacturer's arbitration programs certified under FTC Rule 703, in state programs the consumer retains all other rights and remedies existing under law, including civil court action, unless otherwise specified by the state.

Civil Court Action

A consumer may file a formal law suit under the protection granted by the Lemon Law to seek a refund or replacement. The consumer may also use civil court as a second (or third) avenue of recourse if dissatisfied with the result of either or both arbitration(s).

Provisions of civil court action include:
- Legal costs to consumer (some states allow reimbursement if the consumer prevails);
- No time limitation for case resolution;
- Both parties bound by decision;
- Legal counsel required;
- Award can include punitive and other damages in addition to refund/replace, particularly if a cause of action exists under statutes other than Lemon Law.

A consumer who wishes to use civil court should realize the process involves a formal and often costly judicial proceeding. It is therefore advisable to retain legal counsel.

8

THE LEMON LAW PROCESSES...
STEP BY STEP, WHAT TO EXPECT

February 9th - Odometer reading: 7,445 miles
(John's car is still at the dealership)

John submits his demand letter to the manufacturer. Within a week, yet another attempt is made to repair his vehicle. The results are unsatisfactory. As such, John must now move through the Lemon Law process as defined by his state.

(Author's note: Since there are three processes available to John and our purpose is to help you understand each of them, we'll describe the step by step process for each as if John had selected it as his first choice.)

* * * *

Initiating a formal process such as arbitration or legal action is often an intimidating step for a consumer. Many consumers fail to undertake these avenues of recourse because they are confused or lack clear information on how to proceed. Often, they fear that it will take more time and money than they will ultimately gain, so why bother? These feelings are further heightened by the strength and stature of today's automotive manufacturers.

This chapter provides information about what a you may expect to encounter through each of the resolution methods available as previously described. The structure and procedures for every manufacturer's arbitration program differ as do those of state-administered programs. Civil court proceedings as well reflect legal characteristics specific to each state. There are, however, enough procedural commonalties to describe the process generally and familiarize you with what you may expect to encounter.

JOHN SELECTS: MANUFACTURER'S ARBITRATION PROGRAM

Step 1: John has reached an impasse with the manufacturer. He must now obtain an application form to request arbitration. Forms are obtained either from the manufacturer or the arbitration entity. (Contact information for both parties are included in the Appendices.)

Step 2: John completes and mails the application form directly to the arbitration entity. The form requests basic information such as:

- Consumer's Name, Address, Phone Number
- Vehicle Identification Number (VIN)
- Vehicle Problem
- Repair History
- Statement of Consumers' Desired Ruling on Arbitration

John must clearly state all problems he wants the arbitrator to consider. **Problems not specified on the form may not be arbitrated.** He will attach copies of all repair orders and correspondence regarding the vehicle problem. In addition, he should retain copies of the completed form for his records along with original documents such as repair orders.

Step 3: The arbitration entity receives John's application form and records the "official" date of its receipt. Under FTC Rule 703 requirements, a decision must be rendered within 40 days from this date. After the date has been recorded, the arbitration staff reviews the application and determines whether or not it is complete and if the nature of John's complaint is within their jurisdiction.

Step 4: John and the manufacturer are notified via certified letter from the arbitration entity of the acceptance or rejection of the application. The manufacturer may also be requested to provide a written response to John's complaint for later consideration by the arbitrator(s).

Step 5: The arbitration entity schedules a fact-finding meeting (often called a hearing). John and the manufacturer are notified either by phone or mail of the date and location of this meeting. Normally, the meeting is held at a local office of the arbitration entity which is usually convenient to the consumer's home.

Step 6: The meeting is attended by John, the manufacturer's representative and the arbitrator(s). John may request in advance permission to include persons who can support his position such as independent mechanics, witnesses to the vehicle's condition or an attorney.

John and the manufacturer's representative are allotted a specified time to present their case, usually 20-30 minutes each. Documentation, photos, affidavits, previously approved witnesses, etc. may be used in support of either presentation. Following the initial presentation of cases, a specified time is allotted for rebuttal by each party, usually 10 minutes each. The arbitrator(s) may then direct any questions to either party.

Some programs allow the arbitrator(s) to physically inspect and/or test drive the vehicle. John will be advised in advance by the arbitration entity if the program recommends such an inspection so the vehicle is available if needed.

A tape recording or written transcript of the meeting is prepared for documentary purposes and all written documentation becomes part of the official transcript.

Step 7: The arbitrator(s) evaluates all information presented and renders a decision. The decision is delivered to both John and the manufacturer via certified mail. Decisions can include additional no-charge repairs, reimbursement for repairs, refund or replacement, reimbursement for incidental expenses, or other compromises. Under manufacturer's arbitration, a wider latitude of remedy is allowed than under state arbitration provisions. The decision is binding upon the manufacturer. However, the consumer may chose to reject the decision and pursue the matter further. The arbitration entity normally reiterates these consumer rights in its decision letter.

Step 8: The manufacturer is required to comply with the decision within 20 days of its notification. If additional work is required, the manufacturer will contact John to arrange a mutually convenient time. If reimbursement or replacement is required, the manufacturer will advise John when he can expect compliance. If the manufacturer does not make an effort to comply with the decision, John must re-contact the arbitration entity.

Step 9: The arbitration entity contacts John to determine whether or not the manufacturer complied within a timely manner.

JOHN SELECTS: STATE ARBITRATION PROGRAM

Step 1: John requests an application for arbitration from the state's Office of the Attorney General or Consumer Protection Agency. (See **Appendix I** for contact information.) In some instances, these forms are provided at the time of vehicle purchase.

Step 2: John completes and mails the application form to the specified office or agency. Some states have a filing fee which must be submitted along with the application. The form requests basic information such as:

- Consumer's Name, Address, Phone Numbers
- Vehicle Identification Number (VIN)
- Vehicle Problem
- Repair History
- Statement of Consumers' Desired Ruling
  on Arbitration

John clearly states all problems he wants the arbitrator to consider. **Problems not specified on the form may not be arbitrated.** Copies of all repair orders and correspondence regarding the vehicle problem should be attached to the form. In addition, John should retain copies of the completed form for his records along with original documents such as repair orders.

Step 3: The arbitration entity records the "official" date of receipt of the form. State Lemon Law normally specifies the time allowed for the entity to reach a decision - usually 40-60 days. The state board then reviews the application and determines whether or not John has met the statutory requirements established by the state's Lemon Law. For example, they will verify that John had either four unsuccessful repair attempts for the same substantial nonconformity or the vehicle was out of service for a period exceeding 30 calendar days.

Step 4: A certified letter is sent from the state board to John and the manufacturer advising them of the acceptance or rejection of the application. The manufacturer may also be asked to provide a written response to John's complaint for later consideration by the arbitrator(s).

Step 5: The state office or agency schedules a fact-finding hearing. John and the manufacturer are notified either by phone or mail of the date and location of the hearing. Normally, the hearing is held at a local agency office which is convenient to John's home.

Step 6: The meeting is attended by John, the manufacturer's representative and one or more arbitrators. Some states utilize panels of up to three persons. John may request in advance permission to include persons who can support his position such as independent mechanics, witnesses to the vehicle's condition or an attorney.

John and the manufacturer's representative are allotted a specified time to present their case, usually 20-30 minutes each. Documentation, photos, affidavits, previously approved witnesses, etc. may be used in support of either presentation. Following the initial presentation of cases, a specified time is allotted for rebuttal by each party, usually 10 minutes each. The arbitrator(s) may then direct any questions they have to either party.

Physical inspection or test driving of the vehicle is relatively uncommon in state proceedings, but may be requested by the arbitrator(s). A tape recording or written transcript of the hearing is prepared for documentary purposes and all written documentation becomes part of the official transcript.

Step 7: The arbitrator(s) evaluate all information presented and render a decision in writing. The decision is sent via certified mail to both John and the manufacturer. Decisions in state proceedings are either in favor of the consumer or in favor of the manufacturer. In other words, the arbitrator(s) will award either a refund/replacement to the consumer or no further action by the manufacturer. Currently, state arbitration entities do not consider compromise decisions.

Step 8: The manufacturer is required to comply with the decision within the time limitation specified in the decision letter, usually 30-40 calendar days from its date of issuance. The manufacturer or John can appeal the decision through the court system. A statement about the right to appeal is included in the decision letter.

Step 9: State arbitration boards usually do not make follow-up contact with the consumer to insure the manufacturer has complied with the decision. A consumer who has received a decision and not been contacted by the manufacturer regarding compliance actions within the time parameters allowed should contact the state board immediately.

JOHN SELECTS: CIVIL COURT PROCEDURES

Step 1: John contacts an attorney and arranges an initial consultation to discuss his case. The attorney will evaluate the merits of the case, the existing legal provisions and case precedents, and determine whether or not sufficient grounds exist to pursue the matter.

Step 2: It is likely that the attorney will first contact the manufacturer on an informal basis to present the client's demands. Generally, the attorney will approach the manufacturer's corporate attorney(s) and attempt negotiation of a settlement prior to initiation of a lawsuit.

Step 3: If the manufacturer is unresponsive and/or a negotiated settlement cannot be reached, the attorney will file a civil action on John's behalf.

Step 4: The attorneys for both parties may again attempt negotiation prior to the court date. In addition, both attorneys may undertake legal maneuvers to clarify the complaint, the demands, and the facts of the case.

Step 5: A date will be scheduled by the court to hear the case. John, as the plaintiff, will present his case through his attorney, introducing into evidence testimony of John and witnesses, affidavits, pictures, physical evidence, technical reports and any other relevant information.

The manufacturer, as defendant, will respond through its attorney to the plaintiff's case in much the same manner, using testimony, pictures, physical evidence, technical reports and other relevant information.

Step 6: Civil court cases may or may not be heard before a jury. In some states the plaintiff must demand a jury while in others a jury is automatic unless waived. Either a judge or judge and jury will consider the evidence and render a decision.

Subsequently, the court will determine what award, if any, is appropriate under the Lemon Law statute. Under the statutory guidelines of Lemon Laws:

- Relief is usually limited to refund or replacement of the vehicle and related costs such as towing and incidental expenses.

- Some states also include attorney's fees if the plaintiff prevails. If, however, the manufacturer prevails, the plaintiff is responsible for their own attorney's fees.

- Some states permit assessment of punitive damages where the court determines additional monetary compensation is warranted.

- Consequential damages, personal injury and/or property damages, and similar items can be considered by the court under either Lemon Law or other statutory authority.

In summary

Most states define the procedures by which a consumer can pursue relief under their state's Lemon Laws. Many states require that the manufacturer's arbitration program be used first if it complies with the Magnuson-Moss Act (see **Chapter 3**) and has been certified by the state's Attorney General. If not, the laws generally leave the door open for a consumer to use state arbitration and/or civil court first. The laws also permit a consumer who is unhappy with a decision under manufacturer's arbitration to "try again" with state arbitration or in a civil suit.

CONCLUSION

May 1st - Odometer reading: 3 miles

There goes John T. Consumer in his brand new car. His ordeal is over and thanks to the Lemon Law, justice has been served. It will serve you as well.

Knowledge is power.

APPENDIX I

SUMMARY OF STATE LEMON LAW PROVISIONS

AUTHOR'S NOTE: This section is intended to provide a brief summation of the major provisions of each state's Lemon Law in laymen's language. Although the summaries are a helpful tool to consumers in evaluating an individual situation, they cannot be construed as a substitute for the full context of the law or legal guidance. Readers are cautioned to use them only as a guideline and then seek appropriate clarification either from an attorney or a qualified state agency. The author assumes no liability for errors of omission or commission in providing these brief summaries and is not responsible for the consumer's interpretation of their meaning.

The reader should bear in mind that the state Lemon Law creates a cause of legal action. Their intention is to define statutorily when a motor vehicle fails to conform to the manufacturer's warranty. Other existing state laws may provide alternative avenues of relief for some situations.

SUMMARY OF STATE LEMON LAW PROVISIONS

State	Page
Alabama	I - 4
Alaska	I - 5
Arizona	I - 6
Arkansas	I - 7
California	I - 7
Colorado	I - 9
Connecticut	I - 10
Delaware	I - 11
District of Columbia	I - 13
Florida	I - 14
Georgia	I - 15
Hawaii	I - 17
Idaho	I - 18
Illinois	I - 19
Indiana	I - 20
Iowa	I - 22
Kansas	I - 23
Kentucky	I - 24
Louisiana	I - 25
Maine	I - 26
Maryland	I - 27
Massachusetts	I - 28
Michigan	I - 30
Minnesota	I - 31
Mississippi	I - 32
Missouri	I - 34
Montana	I - 35
Nebraska	I - 36

State	Page
Nevada	I - 37
New Hampshire	I - 38
New Jersey	I - 39
New Mexico	I - 41
New York	I - 42
North Carolina	I - 43
North Dakota	I - 45
Ohio	I - 46
Oklahoma	I - 47
Oregon	I - 48
Pennsylvania	I - 49
Rhode Island	I - 50
South Carolina	I - 52
South Dakota	I - 53
Tennessee	I - 54
Texas	I - 55
Utah	I - 57
Vermont	I - 58
Virginia	I - 56
Washington	I - 61
West Virginia	I - 62
Wisconsin	I - 63
Wyoming	I - 64

ALABAMA

(Enrolled Act 90-479)

COVERAGE

Qualifying vehicles must:
- Be new or previously untitled motor vehicles used primarily for personal, family or household use and be intended for use on public highways.
- Be owned by any person or entity entitled by the terms of the warranty to enforce the warranty.

Coverage period is the earlier of:
- One year OR 12,000 miles from original delivery.
- Coverage may be extended to the earlier of 24 months or 24,000 miles from original delivery IF a defect is first reported to the manufacturer during the one year OR 12,000 mile period and a repair is attempted.
- An action must be brought within three years of the original delivery date.

Defect must substantially impair use, market value or safety.

Defect cannot result from alteration, abuse or neglect.

Nonconformity must continue to exist after 3 or more repair attempts plus a final repair opportunity (at least one of which must occur during the first 12 months or 12,000 miles) OR vehicle is out of service for a total of 30 or more calendar days (at least one of which must occur during the first 12 months or 12,000 miles).

CONSUMER PROCEDURES

Consumer must give written notice of the defect to the manufacturer via certified mail detailing the vehicle, the nonconformity, repair history and repair facilities and demand repair of the nonconformity.

Manufacturer is allowed one additional repair attempt.

Consumer must first utilize manufacturer's informal dispute resolution procedure if it complies with federal rules and regulations.

AWARDS

If the consumer prevails, the manufacturer will be required to (at the consumer's option):
- Replace vehicle with a comparable new vehicle; OR
- Refund the full contract price and related purchase charges such as sales tax, license and registration fees, dealer preparation fees, undercoating, transportation, installed options, non-refundable portions of service contracts, all finance charges incurred after the first report of the nonconformity and incidental costs such as alternative transportation.

- Usage will be deducted based on consumer's first written report of nonconformity per the following formula:

$$\text{Purchase Price} \times \frac{\text{\# of Miles/First Report}}{100{,}000}$$

STATE CONTACT INFORMATION

State of Alabama 205/242-7334
Consumer Protection Division 800/824-5274
Office of the Attorney General
11 S. Union Street
Montgomery, Alabama 36130

ALASKA

(Sec. I, Chapter 101, SLA 1984)

COVERAGE

Qualifying vehicles must:
- Be used for personal, family, or household purposes.
- Be purchased or have ownership transferred to and be registered in Alaska.

Coverage period is the earlier of:
- Express warranty period OR one year from original delivery.
- Claim must be initiated within 60 days of expiration of the coverage period.

Defect must substantially impair use or market value.

Defect cannot result from alteration, abuse or neglect.

Nonconformity must continue to exist after 3 or more repair attempts OR vehicle is out of service for a total of 30 or more business days.

CONSUMER PROCEDURES

Consumer must give written notice by certified mail to the manufacturer and the dealer/repairing agent. Notice must state: the vehicle has a defect and describe it; a reasonable number of repair attempts have been made; demand a repair or replacement within 60 days.

Manufacturer is allowed one additional repair attempt within 30 days of receipt of the notice.

Consumer must first utilize manufacturer's informal dispute resolution procedure if it complies with Magnuson-Moss OR the manufacturer offers in writing upon receipt of the consumer demand a process approved by the Alaska Attorney General.

AWARDS

If the consumer prevails, the manufacturer will be required to
(at the consumer's option):
- Replace vehicle; OR
- Refund the original purchase price, registration, transportation fees, dealer preparation, and other options.
    - Usage will be deducted based on depreciation of the vehicle as calculated on a straight line method over seven years.

STATE CONTACT INFORMATION

State of Alaska
Office of the Attorney General
Consumer Protection Section
1031 West Fourth Avenue
Suite 200
Anchorage, Alaska 99501
907/279-0428

ARIZONA

(ARS 44-1261; ARS 44-1265)

COVERAGE

Qualifying vehicles must:
- Be used for transportation of persons and property.
- Be purchased or have ownership transferred during the period of the express warranty.

Coverage period is the earlier of:
- Express warranty period OR one year from original delivery.

Claim must be initiated within six months of expiration of the coverage period.

Defect must substantially impair use and value.

Defect cannot result from alteration, abuse or neglect.

Nonconformity must continue to exist after 4 or more repair attempts OR vehicle is out of service for a total of 30 or more calendar days.

CONSUMER PROCEDURES

Consumer must give written notice of the defect to the manufacturer.
- Manufacturer is allowed one additional repair attempt.
- Consumer must first utilize manufacturer's informal dispute resolution procedure if it complies with FTC Rule 703.

AWARDS

If the consumer prevails, the manufacturer will be required to
(at the consumer's option):
- Replace vehicle; OR
- Refund the original purchase price and collateral charges.
    - Usage will be deducted based on the consumer's first written report of the nonconformity and during any subsequent periods when the vehicle was not out of service for repair.

STATE CONTACT INFORMATION

State of Arizona
Office of the Attorney General
1275 West Washington Street
Phoenix, Arizona 85007
602/542-3702
1/800/352-8431

Secretary of State
State Capitol, West Wing
1700 West Washington
7th Floor
Phoenix, Arizona 85057
602/542-3701
(State Law Library)

ARKANSAS

No Lemon Law

CALIFORNIA

(Amended Song-Beverly Consumer Warranty Act, 1982)

COVERAGE

Qualifying vehicles must:
- Be purchased or leased and used primarily for personal, family or household purposes (including dealer-owned vehicles and demonstrators).

Coverage period is the earlier of:*
- One year OR 12,000 miles from original delivery.

Defect must substantially impair use or value or safety.
- Nonconformity must continue to exist after 4 or more repair attempts OR vehicle is out of service for a cumulative total of 30 or more calendar days.

CONSUMER PROCEDURES

Consumer must give written notice to the manufacturer of the need for repair if the manufacturer has conspicuously advised consumers of this requirement.
- Consumer must first utilize manufacturer's informal dispute resolution procedure if it complies with Magnuson-Moss AND the manufacturer has provided consumer with written notice of the procedure's availability AND procedure has been certified by the state.

AWARDS

If the consumer prevails, the manufacturer will be required to
(at the consumer's option):
- Replace vehicle including taxes, fees and incidental costs attributable to replacement; OR
- Refund original purchase price including transportation charges; manufacturer installed options; collateral charges; incidental charges including but not limited to reasonable repair, towing and rental charges.
    - Usage will be deducted for consumer use prior to the time the vehicle was taken for repair per the following formula:

$$\text{Contract Price} \times \frac{\text{\# of Miles @ 1st Repair}}{120,000}$$

STATE CONTACT INFORMATION

State of California	916/332-3360
Office of the Attorney General	800/952-5225
1515 K Street, Suite 511	(Toll Free in California)
Sacramento, California 94244	800/952-5548
	(TDD in California)
Bureau of Automotive Repair	916/366-5100
California Department of Consumer Affairs	800/952-5210
10240 Systems Parkway	(Toll Free in California)
Sacramento, California 95827	
California Department of Consumer Affairs	916/445-1254
1020 N Street	916/332-1700 (TDD)
Sacramento, California 95814	
(Centralized Consumer Information)	

* The California statute creates a presumption that a consumer is entitled to a refund/replacement if the vehicle meets the criteria described above. Under the terms of the law, if the manufacturer declines such a refund/replacement when demand is made by the consumer, it must be able to successfully "rebut" the presumption. This rebuttal can be based on the fact that the manufacturer was not provided with a reasonable number of repair opportunities; the defect did not substantially impair the vehicle; or the condition resulted from misuse, abuse, damage or improper maintenance.

If a consumer initiates action beyond the period described under "Length of Coverage" *but within the warranty period*, the consumer may still prevail. However, the burden of proof shifts from the manufacturer to the consumer and it is the consumer who must prove that a substantial nonconformity exists that has not been repaired in a reasonable number of attempts.

COLORADO

(Sec. 1, Title 42, Art. 12, Colo. Rev. Stat.)

COVERAGE

Qualifying vehicles must:
- Be normally used for personal, family or household purposes.
- Be sold in Colorado or have ownership transferred during the express warranty.

Coverage period is the earlier of:
- Express warranty period OR one year from original delivery.
- Action must be brought within the earlier of express warranty period or one year from original delivery.

Defect must substantially impair use and market value and render vehicle nonconforming to the manufacturer's warranty.

Defect cannot result from alteration, abuse or neglect.

Nonconformity must continue to exist after 4 or more repair attempts OR vehicle is out of service for a cumulative total of 30 or more business days (days when dealer conducts business.)

CONSUMER PROCEDURES

Consumer must give written notice by certified mail to the manufacturer if this requirement is conspicuously disclosed and the consumer is provided a form to do so.

Manufacturer is allowed one additional repair attempt which can be counted as one of the necessary 4 repair attempts.

Consumer must first utilize manufacturer's informal dispute resolution procedure if it complies with Magnuson-Moss.

AWARDS

If the consumer prevails, the manufacturer will be required to (at the manufacturer's option):
- Replace vehicle with a comparable vehicle; OR
- Refund the original purchase price and collateral charges including sales tax, license, registration, similar governmental charges.
    - Usage will be deducted based on the amount directly attributable to consumer use prior to the first report of the nonconformity and during subsequent periods when the vehicle was not out of service for repair.

STATE CONTACT INFORMATION

State of Colorado
Consumer Protection Unit
Office of the Attorney General
1525 Sherman Street, 3rd Floor
Denver, Colorado 80203
303/866-5167

CONNECTICUT

(Pub. Acts 82-287; 83-458; 84-338; 85-331)

COVERAGE

Qualifying vehicles must:
- Be passenger or passenger/commercial vehicles.
- Be purchased or leased in Connecticut or have ownership transferred during the express warranty.

Coverage period is the earlier of:
- Two years OR 18,000 miles from original delivery.

Defect must substantially impair use, safety or value.

Defect cannot result from alteration, abuse or neglect.

Nonconformity must continue to exist after 4 or more repair attempts (2 or more if condition is likely to cause death or serious bodily injury) OR vehicle is out of service for a cumulative total of 30 or more calendar days.

CONSUMER PROCEDURES

Consumer must give written notice to the manufacturer *if* the manufacturer has clearly and conspicuously disclosed this requirement to the consumer and provided an address.

No additional repair attempt by the manufacturer required.

Consumer must first utilize manufacturer's informal dispute resolution procedure if it complies with Magnuson-Moss AND has been certified by the Connecticut Attorney General.

Arbitration is also offered by the State of Connecticut for a $50.00 fee (contact address below).

Consumer may use state program prior to court action but is not required to do so. If manufacturer's program is certified by the state, consumer *must* utilize it prior to court action.

AWARDS

If the consumer prevails, the manufacturer will be required to (at the arbitrator's option/decision):
- Replace vehicle; OR
- Refund the original purchase price, transportation fees, dealer options, collateral charges, finance charges after first report of nonconformity and when out of service for repair, incidental damages.
    - Usage can be deducted based on consumer use prior to return per the following formula (arbitrator's discretion):

$$\text{Contract Price} \times \frac{\text{\# of Miles}}{100{,}000}$$

STATE CONTACT INFORMATION

State of Connecticut
Department of Consumer Protection Attention: Lemon Law
165 Capitol Avenue
Hartford, Connecticut 06106
1/800-538-CARS (Toll Free) 203/566-7002

--- ◇ ---

DELAWARE

(Title VI, Ch. 49, S.B. 276)

COVERAGE

Qualifying vehicles must:
- Be new passenger vehicles primarily used on public highways.
- Be registered in Delaware or have ownership transferred during the express warranty.

Coverage period is the earlier of:

- Express warranty period OR one year from original delivery.

Defect must substantially impair use or value or safety.

Defect cannot result from alteration, abuse or neglect.

Nonconformity must continue to exist after 4 or more repair attempts OR vehicle is out of service for a total of 30 or more business days.

CONSUMER PROCEDURES

Consumer must give written notice of the defect to the manufacturer.

Manufacturer is allowed one additional repair attempt.

Consumer must first utilize manufacturer's informal dispute resolution procedure if it complies with Magnuson-Moss AND the Division of Consumer Affairs has issued a Certificate of Approval to the procedure.

AWARDS

If the consumer prevails, the manufacturer will be required to
(at the consumer's option):
- Replace vehicle with a comparable new vehicle including incidental costs such as dealer preparation, fee for registration or transfer, sales tax or other charges incurred as a result of the replacement. Manufacturer shall not require consumer to enter into a financing agreement which creates a greater obligation than the original agreement; OR
- Refund the original purchase price and related purchase charges such as sales tax, registration fees, and dealer preparation fees.
    - Usage will be deducted based on consumer's first written report of nonconformity per the following formula:

$$\text{Purchase Price} \times \frac{\text{\# of Miles/First Report}}{100,000}$$

STATE CONTACT INFORMATION

State of Delaware
Division of Consumer Affairs
Department of Community Affairs
820 North French Street
Wilmington, Delaware 19801
302/577-3250

I-13

DISTRICT OF COLUMBIA

(D.C. Act 5-227)

COVERAGE

Qualifying vehicles must:
- Be passenger vehicles designed for streets, roads, highways.
- Be manufactured, offered for sale, sold, leased, registered in District of Columbia or transferred to District of Columbia during warranty period.

Coverage period is the earlier of:
- Two years OR 18,000 miles from original delivery.

Action must be initiated within 4 years of original delivery.

Defect must substantially impair vehicle.

Defect cannot result from alteration, abuse or neglect.

Nonconformity must continue to exist after 4 or more repair attempts (1 or more if condition is safety-related) OR vehicle is out of service for a cumulative total of 30 or more days for any nonconformity.

CONSUMER PROCEDURES

Consumer must give written notice to the manufacturer if this requirement was clearly and conspicuously disclosed to the consumer by the manufacturer or dealer.

No additional repair attempt by the manufacturer required.

Consumer must utilize D.C. Board of Consumer Claims prior to initiating court action regardless of whether or not the manufacturer offers an informal dispute resolution mechanism. Information may be obtained from address below; filing fee is $25.00.
(Note: Consumer may use manufacturer's program at his option.)

AWARDS

If the consumer prevails, the manufacturer will be required to
(at the consumer's option):
- Replace vehicle with comparable vehicle; OR
- Refund the original purchase price and sales tax, license fees, registration fees, similar governmental charges.
- Usage may be deducted not to exceed 10 cents per mile for consumer use in excess of the first 12,000 miles of operation.

STATE CONTACT INFORMATION

District of Columbia
Department of Consumer and Regulatory Affairs
614 H Street, N.W.
Washington, D.C. 20001
202/727-7000

I-14

FLORIDA

(Chap. 83-69; 85-240; 84-55; 681)

COVERAGE
Qualifying vehicles must:
- Be passenger vehicles used primarily for personal, family or household purposes or commercial vehicles.
- Be sold or leased and operated in Florida or transferred during the manufacturer's warranty. (Leased vehicles are covered only if the lessee is responsible for repairs or if the vehicle is leased under a lease-purchase agreement.)

Coverage period is the earlier of:
- One year OR 12,000 miles from original delivery. (May be be extended if condition is reported and not repaired prior to the end of the period.)
- Action must be brought within one year of period of coverage or 30 days following decision of certified dispute resolution procedure.

Defect must substantially impair use, market value or safety.

Defect cannot result from abuse, neglect or alteration.

Nonconformity must continue to exist after 3 or more repair attempts OR vehicle is out of service for a cumulative total of 20 or more calendar days for one or more nonconformities.

CONSUMER PROCEDURES
Consumer must give written notice to the manufacturer of the defect via registered or express mail.

Manufacturer is allowed one additional repair attempt within 14 days and must notify consumer of repair facility within 7 days of receipt of notification.

Consumer must first utilize manufacturer's informal dispute resolution procedure if it has been certified by the state as substantially complying with Magnuson-Moss.

Consumer has relief under Florida New Motor Vehicle Arbitration Board ($50.00 filing fee) if:
- Manufacturer's mechanism has not rendered a decision within time limits specified in FTC 703.
- Consumer is not satisfied with decision of manufacturer's mechanism.
- Manufacturer has no state-certified mechanism.

Consumer must submit dispute to state board prior to filing in civil court.

Information may be obtained through the address listed below.

AWARDS
If the consumer prevails, the manufacturer will be required to (at the consumer's option):

Purchased Vehicles:
- Replace vehicle with comparable vehicle; OR
- Refund purchase price including reasonably incurred collateral and incidental charges.
- Usage deduction for reasonable use calculated by multiplying number of miles driven prior to the third report of the nonconformity or the 20th out of service day by the price of the vehicle and divided by 120,000.

Leased Vehicles:
- Lessee receives aggregate of deposit and rental payments paid to lessor less the usage deduction (above).
- Lessor receives aggregate of lessee's actual purchase price; collateral charges; fees paid to obtain lease; insurance or other costs expended on lessee's behalf; state and local taxes; and an amount equal to 5 percent of the purchase price less the aggregate deposit and rental payments received from the lessee.

STATE CONTACT INFORMATION

State of Florida
Department of Agriculture and Consumer Services
The Mayo Building, Room 208
Tallahassee, FL 32399-0800
800/321-5366

--- ◆ ---

GEORGIA

(Motor Vehicle Warranty Rights Act-Effective January 2, 1991)

COVERAGE

Qualifying vehicles must:
- Be new vehicles, demonstrator or lease-purchase vehicles as long as manufacturer's warranty is issued.
- Be purchased, leased or registered by the original consumer in the state of Georgia after June 30, 1990.

Coverage period is the earlier of:
- One year OR 12,000 miles from original delivery.
- If first repair or 15 days out of service are documented during one year/12,000 miles, consumer may accrue additional repair attempts/days up to 24 months/24,000 miles.
- Action must be brought within the later of 30 months from original delivery or

18 months after expiration of the 12 month/12,000 miles Lemon Law period.
Defect must substantially impair use, value or safety.
Defect cannot result from abuse, neglect or alteration.
Nonconformity must continue to exist after:
- 1 repair attempt for serious safety defect in braking or steering system during 12 months/12,000 miles; OR
- 2 or more repair attempts for serious defect during 24 months/24,000 miles if at least one attempt was during 12 month/12,000 mile period; OR
- 3 or more repair attempts for a nonconformity within 24 months/24,000 miles if at least one attempt was during 12 month/12,000 mile period; OR
- Vehicle is out of service for a cumulative total of 30 or more calendar days if at least 15 days were within 12 month/12,000 mile period.

CONSUMER PROCEDURES

Consumer must give written notice to the manufacturer of the defect via certified mail, return receipt requested if this requirement was stated at time of purchase.

Manufacturer is allowed one additional repair attempt within 14 days and must notify consumer of repair facility within 7 days of receipt of notification.

Consumer must first utilize manufacturer's informal dispute resolution procedure if it has been certified by the state AND substantially complies with Magnuson-Moss.

Consumer has relief under state-administered arbitration board if dissatisfied with decision rendered by manufacturer's board or the manufacturer does not offer a state-certified mechanism. Consumer must utilize state-administered board prior to initiating court action.

Information may be obtained through the address listed below.

AWARDS

If the consumer prevails, the manufacturer will be required to
(at the consumer's option):
Purchased Vehicles:
- Replace vehicle with comparable vehicle including all collateral charges incurred as a result of the replacement and incidental costs less a usage deduction; OR
- Refund purchase price and reasonably incurred collateral charges such as manufacturer or dealer installed items and service charges; earned financce charges; sales tax and title charges and incidental costs less a usage deduction.
- Usage deduction for reasonable use prior to written notice to manufacturer per the following formula:

$$\frac{\text{\# of Miles } \times \text{ Purchase Price}}{100,000}$$

Leased Vehicles:
- Refunds include items listed under purchase refunds (above) and the consumer's lease agreement is to be terminated with no penalty assessed for early termination.

STATE CONTACT INFORMATION

State of Georgia	Governor's Office of Consumer
Clerk's Office	Affairs
State Capitol - Room 309	2 Martin Luther King Dr., SE
Atlanta, Georgia 30334	Plaza Level, East Tower
404/656-5015	Atlanta, Georgia 30334
	404/656-1760
	800/282-5808
	(State Arbitration Board)

HAWAII

(490:2-313.1)

COVERAGE

Qualifying vehicles must:
- Be vehicles used primarily for personal, family or household purposes.
- Be new vehicles, including demonstrators, sold or leased with a manufacturer's warranty.

Coverage period is the express warranty period.

Action must be brought within one year of expiration of the express warranty.

Defect must substantially impair use, value or safety.

Defect cannot result from abuse, neglect or alteration.

Nonconformity must continue to exist after 3 or more repair attempts OR vehicle is out of service for a cumulative total of 30 or more business days.

CONSUMER PROCEDURES

Consumer must give written notice to the manufacturer of the defect if the manufacturer has provided the consumer with written notice of the state arbitration program and the consumer's rights under the law.

Manufacturer is allowed one additional repair attempt upon receipt of the consumer's written notice.

Consumer may first utilize manufacturer's informal dispute resolution procedure or the state arbitration board.

Information on state arbitration board may be obtained through address listed below; $50.00 filing fee.

AWARDS
- If the consumer prevails, the manufacturer will be required to
    (at the consumer's option):
    - Replace vehicle with comparable vehicle; OR
    - Refund original purchase price and all collateral and incidental charges including but not limited to sales tax, excise tax, license fees, registration, title charges, towing charges, rental costs.
    - Usage deduction for reasonable use prior to first report of the nonconformity based on one percent of the purchase price for every thousand miles of use.

STATE CONTACT INFORMATION

State of Hawaii
Office of Consumer Affairs
828 Fort Street Mall
Post Office Box 3767
Honolulu, Hawaii 96812-3767
808/548-2520

American Arbitration Association
810 Richards Street, Suite 641
Honolulu, Hawaii 96813
808/531-0541
Telecopier: 808/533-2306
(State Arbitration Board)

IDAHO

(Chapter 9, Title 48)

COVERAGE

Qualifying vehicles must:
- Be used for personal, family, or household purposes.
- Be sold in the state of Idaho.

Coverage period is the earlier of:
- One year OR 12,000 miles from original delivery.

Defect must substantially impair use, market value or safety.

Defect cannot result from alteration, abuse or neglect.

Nonconformity must continue to exist after 4 or more repair attempts OR vehicle is out of service for a cumulative total of 30 or more business days.

CONSUMER PROCEDURES

Consumer must give written notice of the defect to the manufacturer.
No provision exists for an additional repair attempt by the manufacturer.

Consumer must first utilize manufacturer's informal dispute resolution procedure if it complies with Magnuson-Moss.

AWARDS

If the consumer prevails, the manufacturer will be required to
(at the consumer's option):
- Replace vehicle; OR
- Refund the original purchase price and all collateral charges.
    - Usage will be deducted based on consumer use prior to the first report of the nonconformity and subsequent periods when the vehicle was not out of service based on the current Internal Revenue Service deduction for business use of an automobile.

STATE CONTACT INFORMATION

State of Idaho
Consumer Protection
Office of the Attorney General
State House, Room 113A
Boise, Idaho   83720
208/334-2424

ILLINOIS

(Public Act 87-768)

COVERAGE

Qualifying vehicles must:
- Be new motor vehicles having a weight of under 8,000 pounds including recreational vehicles purchased primarily for personal and family purposes.
- Be used for personal, family, or household purposes.
- Be replacement vehicles received under Lemon Law.

Coverage period is the earlier of:
- One year OR 12,000 miles from original delivery.
- Action must be initiated within 18 months of the original delivery date.

Defect must substantially impair use, market value or safety.

Defect cannot result from alteration, abuse or neglect.

Nonconformity must continue to exist after 4 or more repair attempts OR vehicle is out of service for a cumulative total of 30 or more business days.

CONSUMER PROCEDURES

Consumer must give written notice of the defect to the manufacturer.

The manufacuturer is allowed a final opportunity to repair the defect.

Consumer must first utilize manufacturer's informal dispute resolution procedure if it complies with Magnuson-Moss; AND

- The manufacturer provides adequate written notice of the procedure to the consumer; AND
- The decision under that procedure explains to the consumer provisions about his/her right to bring further civil court action and the admissibility of the arbitration decision.

AWARDS

If the consumer prevails, the manufacturer will be required to:

- Replace vehicle; OR
- Refund the original purchase price and all collateral charges.
    - Usage will be deducted based on consumer use prior to the first report of the nonconformity and during subsequent periods when the vehicle was not out of service for repair.

STATE CONTACT INFORMATION

State of Illinois
Office of the Attorney General - Consumer Protection Division
100 West Randolph, 12th Floor
Chicago, Illinois 60601
312/814-3580; 800/252-8666; 312/814-7123 (TDD)

INDIANA

(P.L. 88-150, Sec. 1)

COVERAGE

Qualifying vehicles must:
- Be intended primarily for use and operation on public highways.
- Be purchased or leased or transferred or replaced in Indiana. Effective 9/1/90, coverage is extended to non-residents who purchase vehicles in the state.

Coverage period is the earlier of:
- Eighteen months OR 18,000 miles from original delivery.
- Action must be initiated within 2 years of the first report of the defect to the manufacturer/dealer.

Defect must substantially impair use, market value or safety.

Defect must render vehicle nonconforming to warranty.

Defect cannot result from alteration, abuse or neglect.

Nonconformity must continue to exist after 4 or more repair attempts OR vehicle is out of service for a cumulative total of 30 or more business days for the nonconformity.

CONSUMER PROCEDURES

Consumer must give written notice of the defect to the manufacturer if manufacturer has disclosed this requirement clearly and conspicuously.

No provision for an additional repair attempt.

Consumer must first utilize manufacturer's informal dispute resolution procedure if it complies with Magnuson-Moss; AND
- The manufacturer provides adequate written notice of the procedure to the consumer; AND
- The procedure has been certified by the Attorney General.

AWARDS

If the consumer prevails, the manufacturer will be required to
(at the consumer's option):
- Replace vehicle including reimbursement of actual towing and rental costs incurred by the consumer due to nonconformity; OR
- Refund the original purchase price and all collateral charges including sales tax, unexpended portion of the registration fee/excise tax; finance charges actually expended; dealer options; towing and rental costs incurred by the consumer due to nonconformity.
    - Usage will be deducted per the following formula:

    $$\text{Contract Price} \times \frac{\text{\# Miles/Time of Repurchase}}{100,000}$$

- Lessees will receive a refund of all deposit and lease payments made including trade-in credit/allowance less usage deduction as noted above. In addition, the lessor will receive a refund based on the purchase cost including freight and accessories, fees paid to obtain lease, insurance premiums and other costs expended, sales tax and 5% of the purchase cost LESS the amount previously received from the lessee.

STATE CONTACT INFORMATION

State of Indiana
Office of the Attorney General
Consumer Protection Division
219 State House
Indianapolis, Indiana 46204
317/232-6330 800/382-5516 (Toll Free in Indiana)

IOWA

(Iowa Code Chapter 322E)

COVERAGE

Qualifying vehicles must:
- Be used for personal, family, household or agricultural purposes.
- Be purchased in Iowa or have ownership transferred during the warranty period.

Coverage period is the earlier of:
- Express warranty period OR one year from original delivery.
- Action must be initiated within the earlier of 6 months from expiration of the express warranty period or 6 months following one year after original delivery.

Defect must substantially impair use and value.

Defect cannot result from alteration, abuse or neglect.

Nonconformity must continue to exist after 4 or more repair attempts OR vehicle is out of service for a cumulative total of 30 or more calendar days.

CONSUMER PROCEDURES

Consumer must give written notice of the defect to the manufacturer.

The manufacuturer is allowed a final opportunity to repair the defect upon receipt of the written notice.

Consumer must first utilize manufacturer's informal dispute resolution procedure if it complies with Magnuson-Moss.

AWARDS

If the consumer prevails, the manufacturer will be required to:
- Replace vehicle; OR
- Refund the original purchase price and all collateral charges.
    - Usage will be deducted based on consumer use prior to the first report of the nonconformity and subsequent periods when the vehicle was not out of service for repair.

STATE CONTACT INFORMATION

State of Iowa
Consumer Protection Division
1300 East Walnut
Hoover Building, Second Floor
Des Moines, Iowa 50319
515/281-5926

KANSAS

(L. 1985, Ch. 39, Sec. 2)

COVERAGE

Qualifying vehicles must:
- Be purchased and registered in Kansas.

Coverage period is the earlier of:
- Express warranty period OR one year from original delivery.
- Coverage period may be extended if a consumer reports a defect to a manufacturer during the one year OR express warranty period and the defect is not corrected.

Defect must substantially impair use and value.

Defect cannot result from alteration, abuse or neglect.

Nonconformity must continue to exist after 4 or more repair attempts OR vehicle is out of service for a cumulative total of 30 or more calendar days OR 10 or more repair attempts are performed for non-related nonconformities.

CONSUMER PROCEDURES

Consumer must give written notice of the defect to the manufacturer.

No provision for an additional repair attempt by the manufacturer.

Consumer must first utilize manufacturer's informal dispute resolution procedure if it complies with Magnuson-Moss.

AWARDS

If the consumer prevails, the manufacturer will be required to:
- Replace vehicle; OR
- Refund the original purchase price and all collateral charges.
    - Usage will be deducted based on consumer use prior to the first report of the nonconformity and subsequent periods when the vehicle was not out of service for repair and calculated on the basis of most recent AAA "Your Driving Costs."

STATE CONTACT INFORMATION

State of Kansas
Consumer Protection Division
Office of the Attorney General
Kansas Judicial Center, 2nd Floor
Topeka, Kansas 66612

913/296-3751
800/432-2310 (Toll Free in Kansas)

KENTUCKY

(K.R.S. 367.840 to 367.845)

COVERAGE

Qualifying vehicles must:
- Be intended primarily for use and operation on public highways.
- Be purchased and required to be registered in Kentucky.

Coverage period is the earlier of:
- Twelve months OR 12,000 miles from original delivery.
- Action must be brought within 2 years of original delivery.

Defect must substantially impair use, value or safety.

Defect cannot result from alteration, abuse or neglect.

Nonconformity must continue to exist after 4 or more repair attempts OR vehicle is out of service for a cumulative total of 30 or more calendar days for repair of the same nonconformity.

CONSUMER PROCEDURES

Consumer must give written notice of the defect to the manufacturer.

No provision for an additional repair attempt by the manufacturer.

Consumer must first utilize manufacturer's informal dispute resolution procedure if it complies with Magnuson-Moss.

AWARDS

If the consumer prevails, the manufacturer will be required to
(at the consumer's option):
- Replace vehicle; OR
- Refund the original purchase price and all collateral charges including sales tax, finance charges, license/ registration fees, similar governmental charges.
- Usage will be deducted based on consumer use of the vehicle other than those time periods when the vehicle was out of service due to the nonconformity.

STATE CONTACT INFORMATION

State of Kentucky 502/564-2200
Office of the Attorney General 800/432-9257 (Toll Free in Kentucky)
Consumer Protection Division
209 Saint Clair Street
Frankfort, Kentucky 40601

LOUISIANA

(Acts 1984 No. 228; Acts 1985 No. 169;
Acts 1986, Nos. 553 and 1058)

COVERAGE

Qualifying vehicles must:
- Be intended for personal, family or household purposes.
- Be purchased or leased in Louisiana or have ownership transferred during the express warranty.

Coverage period is the earlier of:
- Express warranty period OR one year from original delivery.

Defect must substantially impair use and/or market value.

Nonconformity must continue to exist after 4 or more repair attempts OR vehicle is out of service for a cumulative total of 30 or more calendar days.

CONSUMER PROCEDURES

No provision for written notice to the manufacturer.

No provision for an additional repair attempt by the manufacturer.

Consumer must first utilize manufacturer's informal dispute resolution procedure if it complies with Magnuson-Moss.

AWARDS

If the consumer prevails, the manufacturer will be required to
(at the manufacturer's option):

Purchased Vehicles:
- Replace vehicle; OR
- Refund the original purchase price and all collateral charges including sales tax, license/registration fees, similar governmental charges.
    - Usage will be deducted based on consumer use of the vehicle prior to first report of the nonconformity and during subsequent periods when the vehicle was not being repaired.

Leased Vehicles:
- Replace vehicle; OR
- Refund all reasonable expenditures attributable to the lease agreement AND any amount necessary to satisfythe lease obligation including early termination fees.
- Usage will be deducted as described above.

STATE CONTACT INFORMATION

State of Louisiana
Office of the Attorney General
Consumer Protection Section

State Capitol Building
P.O. Box 94005
Baton Rouge, LA 70804
504/342-7013

MAINE

(10 M.R.S.A., Sec. 1161-1169)

COVERAGE

Qualifying vehicles must:
- Be vehicles designed for conveyance of passengers or property on public highways.
- Be purchased or leased in Maine.

Coverage period is the earlier of:
- Two years OR 18,000 miles from original delivery if the nonconformity is reported during the express warranty period.

Defect must substantially impair use, safety or value.

Nonconformity must continue to exist after 3 or more repair attempts (at least two of which must be at the same dealer) OR vehicle is out of service for a cumulative total of 15 or more days for one or more defects.

CONSUMER PROCEDURES

Consumer must give written notice to the manufacturer or dealer via certified mail if the manufacturer has clearly and conspicuously disclosed this requirement and provided the name and address to which the notice must be sent.

Manufacturer is allowed seven business days in which to make a final repair attempt at a reasonably accessible facility.

Prior to initiating court acction, consumer must utilize either the state-administered arbitration procedure or the manufacturer's procedure if it complies with Magnuson-Moss.

Information on the state arbitration procedure is available through the address listed below.

AWARDS

If the consumer prevails, the manufacturer will be required to (at the consumer's option):
- Replace vehicle with comparable vehicle; OR
- Refund original purchase price including all collateral charges such as sales

tax, license/registration fees, similar governmental charges, costs incurred for towing or replacement transportation during repairs.
- Usage deduction for reasonable use per the following formula:
$$\text{Purchase Price} \times \frac{\text{\# of Miles @ Repurchase}}{100,000}$$
- Reasonable attorney's fees may be awarded in civil court.

STATE CONTACT INFORMATION
Attorney General's Lemon Law Arbitration Program
Consumer and Antitrust Division
State House Station 6
Augusta, Maine 04333
207/289-3068

———————— ◆ ————————

MARYLAND

(Ch. 581; Ch. 127; Ch. 750; Ch. 786)

COVERAGE
Qualifying vehicles must:
- Be passenger vehicles, multipurpose vehicles or trucks with less than 3/4 ton capacity.
- Be purchased or leased and registered in Maryland or have ownership transferred during the express warranty.

Coverage period is the earlier of:
- Fifteen months OR 15,000 miles from original delivery.
- An action must be brought within 3 years of delivery.

Defect must substantially impair use and market value.
Defect cannot result from alteration, abuse or neglect.
Nonconformity must continue to exist after 4 or more repair attempts (1 repair for condition involving the failure of the braking or steering system) OR vehicle is out of service for a cumulative total of 30 or more calendar days for one or more defects.

CONSUMER PROCEDURES
Consumer must give written notice to manufacturer by certified mail if the manufacturer has provided a conspicuous statement disclosing this requriement.
The manufacturer is provided an opportunity to resolve the condition.
Use of informal dispute resolution procedure not required.

AWARDS

If the consumer prevails, the manufacturer will be required to:
- Purchased Vehicles
    - Replace vehicle; OR
    - Refund the original purchase price and charges including excise tax, license/registration fees, similar governmental charges.
    - Usage will be deducted based on consumer use of the vehicle not to exceed 15% of the purchase price.
- Leased Vehicles:
    - Replace vehicle or refund purchase price as above; AND
    - Refund all amounts paid to repair vehicle.
- Excise tax is refunded by Motor Vehicle Administration.
- Reasonable attorney's fees may be awarded in court action.

STATE CONTACT INFORMATION

State of Maryland
Office of the Attorney General, Consumer Protection Division
200 St. Paul Place
Baltimore, Maryland 21202
301/528-8662 (9am-3pm); 301/576-6372 (Balt. TDD)
202/470-7534 (Wash. TDD)
800/492-2114, then dial 870-892 (Toll Free in Maryland)

MASSACHUSETTS

(M.G.L. Chapter 90, Section 7N 1/2)

COVERAGE

Qualifying vehicles must:
- Be new vehicles, including demonstrator/executive vehicles.
- Be sold or replaced in Massachusetts or transferred during the express or implied warranties.

Coverage period is the earlier of:
- One year OR 15,000 miles from original delivery (one year OR 15,000 miles from the in-service date for demonstrator/executive vehicles).
- Action must be initiated within 18 months from original delivery date.

Defect must substantially impair use, market value or safety.

Defect cannot result from negligence, accident, vandalism, repair attempt by other than manufacturer/dealer or substantial unauthorized modification.

I-29

Nonconformity must continue to exist after 3 or more repair attempts (within one year/15,000 miles) OR vehicle is out of service for a cumulative total of 15 or more business days.

CONSUMER PROCEDURES

The consumer must provide notice to the manufacturer.

Manufacturer is allowed seven business days in which to make a final repair attempts upon receipt of consumer notice.

Massachusetts provides state-certified new car arbitration through the state.

The consumer is not obligated to use the manufacturer's procedure prior to the state program.

Information on the state arbitration procedure is available through the address listed below.

AWARDS

If the consumer prevails, the manufacturer will be required to:
- Replace vehicle with comparable vehicle; OR
- Refund original purchase price including collateral charges such as sales tax, registration fees, finance charges, costs of dealer-added options and incidental charges.
    - Usage deduction for reasonable use per the following formula:

        $$\frac{\text{Contract Price}}{100,000} \times \text{\# Miles/Time of Repurchase}$$

- Incidental fees may be awarded at arbitrator's discretion.
- When vehicle is financed by manufacturer or its subsidiary no increased financial obligation may be created.
- Consumer can reject replacement and demand a refund.

STATE CONTACT INFORMATION

State of Massachusetts, Lemon Law Arbitration Program
Executive Office of Consumer Affairs
One Ashburton Place, Room 1411
Boston, Massachusetts 02108
617/727-4061 (Arbitration Info); 617/727-7780 (General Info)

I-30

MICHIGAN

(P.L. 1986, No. 87)

COVERAGE

Qualifying vehicles must:
- Be intended for use as a passenger vehicle for personal, family or household purposes.
- Be purchased in or by a Michigan resident.

Coverage period is the earlier of:
- Express warranty period or one year from original delivery.

Defect must substantially impair use or value and render vehicle nonconforming to applicable manufacturer's warranty.

Defect cannot result from alteration, abuse or neglect.

Nonconformity must continue to exist after 4 or more repair attempts OR vehicle is out of service for a cumulative total of 30 or more business days (or parts of days) for any nonconformity.

CONSUMER PROCEDURES

Consumer must give written notice of the defect to the manufacturer via certified mail, return-receipt requested after third repair or 25th out of service day.

The manufacturer is provided an additional repair attempt to be completed within 5 business days after consumer delivers vehicle to a reasonably accessible repair facility.

Consumer must first utilize manufacturer's informal dispute resolution procedure if it complies with Magnuson-Moss AND is binding upon manufacturer AND allows consumer redress through civil court or other means.

AWARDS

If the consumer prevails, the manufacturer will be required to (at the manufacturer's option):
- Replace vehicle; OR
- Refund the original purchase price and cost of options or modifications by manufacturer, all other charges made by or for manufacturer, and all necessary towing and rental costs actually incurred that resulted directly from the nonconformity.
- Usage will be deducted at a rate of 10 cents per mile or 10 percent of the purchase price, whichever is less, for mileage at the first report of the nonconformity.

I-31

STATE CONTACT INFORMATION
Michigan Department of the Attorney General
Consumer Protection Division
P.O. Box 30213
Lansing, Michigan 48909
517/373-1140

MINNESOTA

(325F.665)

COVERAGE

Qualifying vehicles must:
- Be new vehicles used at least 40% for personal, family or household purposes.
- Be sold or leased to a consumer in Minnesota or transferred during the express warranty. (Awards for lessees are limited to return of vehicle, lease termination and refund of amount paid by consumer.)

Coverage period is the earlier of:
- Express warranty or two years from original delivery.
- Action must be brought within 3 years of delivery date if consumer originally notified manufacturer during express warranty OR 6 months from final decision of dispute resolution mechanism.

Defect must substantially impair use or market value.

Defect cannot result from alteration, abuse or neglect.

Nonconformity must continue to exist after 4 or more repair attempts (1 repair attempt for defect which results in failure of braking or steering systems likely to cause serious injury/death) OR vehicle is out of service for a cumulative total of 30 or more business days for any nonconformity.

CONSUMER PROCEDURES

Consumer must give written notice of the defect to the manufacturer.

The manufacturer is provided an additional repair attempt after receipt of the written notification.

Manufacturer must provide informal dispute settlement mechanism.

Mechanism must be used prior to civil action unless the manufacturer allows consumer to proceed directly to court.

Application to district court to remove mechanism's decision must be made within 30 days of decision.

AWARDS

If the consumer prevails, the manufacturer will be required to:

Purchased Vehicles:
- Replace vehicle including trade-in value of consumer's used vehicle and additional amount paid for new vehicle or lease cost; OR
- Refund the original purchase price, manufacturer or dealer installed options, modifications made within 30 days of delivery, excise tax, license/registration fees, towing and rental expenses (if applicable).
- Usage will be deducted at a rate of 10 cents per mile or 10 percent of the purchase price, whichever is less, for mileage directly attributable to consumer when vehicle was not substantially impaired.

Leased Vehicles:
- Termination of lease agreement;
- Full refund of amount actually paid by consumer on written lease including all charges as specified above;
- Refund to lessor of full purchase price and early termination charges not to exceed 15 percent of original purchase price less amount paid by consumer.

Special Note

The length of coverage cited above does not preclude an award to a consumer who can show a reasonable number of repair attempts within three years following original delivery provided the first report was during the express warranty period.

STATE CONTACT INFORMATION

State of Minnesota
Office of the Attorney General
Office of Consumer Services
117 University Avenue
St. Paul, Minnesota 55155
612/296-3353

---------------- ◆ ----------------

MISSISSIPPI

(Sec. 63-17-151, et. seq.)

COVERAGE

Qualifying vehicles must:
- Be intended for use primarily for personal, family or household purposes.
- Be purchased in Mississippi.

- Be demonstrators or lease-purchase vehicles if a manufacturer's warranty was issued as sale condition.

Coverage period is the earlier of:
- Express warranty period or one year from original delivery. (May be extended for defect reported within time limit but not repaired.)
- Action must be brought within the earlier of 18 months from delivery or one year after warranty expiration OR within 90 days of final action of informal dispute settlement proceeding.

Defect must substantially impair use, market value or safety.

Defect cannot result from alteration, abuse or neglect.

Nonconformity must continue to exist after 3 or more repair attempts OR vehicle is out of service for a cumulative total of 15 or more working days.

CONSUMER PROCEDURES

Consumer must give written notice of the defect to the manufacturer.
- The manufacturer must notify consumer of a reasonably accessible repair facility upon receipt of notice and then has 10 calendar days to repair vehicle after the consumer delivers it to the facility.
- Consumer must first utilize manufacturer's informal dispute resolution procedure if it complies with Magnuson-Moss.

AWARDS

If the consumer prevails, the manufacturer will be required to (at the consumer's option):
- Replace vehicle; OR
- Refund the original purchase price and collateral charges including dealer preparation, undercoating, transportation, towing and replacement rental car, title charges.
- Usage will be deducted from both replacement/refund based on the number of miles driven at 20 cents per mile.

STATE CONTACT INFORMATION

State of Mississippi
Office of the Attorney General - Consumer Protection Division
P.O. Box 220
Jackson, Mississippi 39205
601/354-6018

MISSOURI

(Ch. 407.506 - 407.579)

COVERAGE

Qualifying vehicles must:
- Be intended for use primarily for personal, family or household purposes.
- Be purchased or transferred during express warranty period.
- Be demonstrators or lease-purchase vehicles if a manufacturer's warranty was issued as sale condition.

Coverage period is the earlier of:
- Express warranty period or one year from original delivery. (May be extended for defect reported within time limit but not repaired.)
- Action must be brought within the earlier of 18 months from delivery or one year after warranty expiration OR within 90 days of final action of informal dispute settlement proceeding.

Defect must substantially impair use, market value or safety.

Defect cannot result from alteration, abuse or neglect.

Nonconformity must continue to exist after 4 or more repair attempts OR vehicle is out of service for a cumulative total of 30 or more working days.

CONSUMER PROCEDURES

Consumer must give written notice of the defect to the manufacturer if the manufacturer has provided the consumer with written information about complaint remedies at the time of purchase.
- The manufacturer must notify consumer of a reasonably accessible repair facility upon receipt of notice and then has 10 calendar days to repair vehicle after consumer delivery to this facility.
- Consumer must first utilize manufacturer's informal dispute resolution procedure if it complies with Magnuson-Moss.

AWARDS

- If the consumer prevails, the manufacturer will be required to (at the manufacturer's option):
    - Replace vehicle; OR
    - Refund the original purchase price and collateral charges including sales tax, license fees, registration fees, title fees, motor vehicle inspections.
- Usage will be deducted from both replacement/refund.
- Reasonable attorney's fees may be awarded in court action.

I-35

STATE CONTACT INFORMATION
State of Missouri
Office of the Attorney General; Trade Offense Division
P.O. Box 899
Jefferson City, Missouri 65102
314/751-3630; 1/800/392-8222 (Toll Free in Missouri)

———————— ◆ ————————

MONTANA

(Mont. Code Ann. 61-4-501; Ch. 744; Ch. 144)

COVERAGE

Qualifying vehicles must:
- Be intended for transportation of persons or property.
- Be sold in Montana or transferred during express warranty period.

Coverage period is the earlier of:
- Two years OR 18,000 miles from original delivery.

Defect must substantially impair use and market value or safety.

Defect cannot result from alteration, abuse or neglect.

Nonconformity must continue to exist after 4 or more repair attempts OR vehicle is out of service for a cumulative total of 30 or more business days.

CONSUMER PROCEDURES

Consumer must give written notice of the defect to the manufacturer if the manufacturer has provided notice of this requirement.

The manufacturer is provided an additional repair attempt upon receipt of written notice.

Consumer must first utilize manufacturer's informal dispute resolution procedure if it complies with Magnuson-Moss AND has been certified by the Department of Commerce.

A state arbitration panel is available if the manufacturer does not have a certified procedure. Information is available through the address listed below; $50.00 filing fee.

AWARDS

If the consumer prevails, the manufacturer will be required to:
- Replace vehicle; OR
- Refund the original purchase price and collateral charges including sales tax,

license fees, registration fees, similar governmental fees, incidental and consequential damages which can include reasonable expenses incurred in inspection, transportation and storage of vehicle, purchase of a substitute vehicle, any loss the dealer/ manufacturer had reason to anticipate, personal injury and property damages.

- Usage will be deducted per the following formula:

$$\text{Contract Price} \times \frac{\text{\# Miles at Repurchase}}{100,000}$$

STATE CONTACT INFORMATION

State of Montana
Department of Commerce; Consumer Affairs Unit
1424 North Avenue
Helena, Montana 59620
406/444-4312

NEBRASKA

(Neb. Rev. Stat. Secs. 60-2701 through 60-2709)

COVERAGE

Qualifying vehicles must:
- Be intended primarily for personal, family or household use.
- Be purchased or have ownership transferred during the express warranty period.

Coverage period is the earlier of:
- One year from delivery OR express warranty period.
- Action must be brought within 2 years from original delivery or one year after expiration of express warranty.

Defect must substantially impair use and market value.

Defect cannot result from alteration, abuse or neglect.

Nonconformity must continue to exist after 4 or more repair attempts OR vehicle is out of service for a cumulative total of 40 or more calendar days for repair.

CONSUMER PROCEDURES

Consumer must give written notice of the defect to the manufacturer by certified mail.
- The manufacturer is allowed one additional repair opportunity.
- Consumer must first utilize manufacturer's informal dispute resolution procedure if it complies with Magnuson-Moss AND has been certified by the Director of Motor Vehicles.

I-37

AWARDS
- If the consumer prevails, the manufacturer will be required to (at the consumer's option):
    - Replace vehicle; OR
    - Refund the original purchase price and all collateral charges including sales tax, license/registration fees, similar governmental charges.
        - Usage will be deducted based on consumer use of the vehicle prior to the first report of the nonconformity and during subsequent periods when the vehicle was not out of service for repair.

STATE CONTACT INFORMATION
State of Nebraska
Office of the Attorney General
Consumer Protection Division
Department of Justice
2115 State Capitol
P.O. Box 94906
Lincoln, Nebraska 68509
402/471-2682

Department of Motor Vehicles
P.O. Box 94789
Lincoln, Nebraska 68509
402/471-3904

———————— ◆ ————————

NEVADA

(NRS 598.751 to 598.791)

COVERAGE
Qualifying vehicles must:
- Be intended primarily for personal, family or household use.
- Be purchased or have ownership transferred during the express warranty period.

Coverage period is the earlier of:
- One year from delivery OR express warranty period.
- Action must be brought within 18 months of original delivery date.

Defect must substantially impair use and value.

Defect cannot result from alteration, abuse or neglect.

Nonconformity must continue to exist after 4 or more repair attempts OR vehicle is out of service for a cumulative total of 30 or more calendar days for any nonconformity.

CONSUMER PROCEDURES

Consumer must give written notice of the defect to the manufacturer before expiration of one year from delivery or the express warranty period, whichever is earlier.

No provision is included for an additional repair opportunity.

Consumer must first utilize manufacturer's informal dispute resolution procedure if it complies with Magnuson-Moss.

AWARDS

If the consumer prevails, the manufacturer will be required to:
- Replace vehicle with the same model and features; OR
- Refund the original purchase price and all collateral charges including sales tax, license/registration fees, similar governmental charges.
    - Usage will be deducted based on consumer use of the vehicle prior to the first report of the nonconformity and during subsequent periods when the vehicle was not out of service for repair.

STATE CONTACT INFORMATION

State of Nevada
Office of Consumer Affairs
Department of Commerce
State Mail Room Complex
Las Vegas, Nevada 89158
702/486-4150

NEW HAMPSHIRE

(RSA Ch. 357-D, Consumer Motor Vehicle Warranties)

COVERAGE

Qualifying vehicles must:
- Be private passenger or station wagon type vehicles.
- Be purchased or have ownership transferred during the express warranty period in New Hampshire.

Coverage period is the earlier of:
- One year from delivery OR express warranty period.

Defect must substantially impair use and value and render the vehicle nonconforming to express or implied warranties.

Defect cannot result from alteration, abuse or neglect.

Nonconformity must continue to exist after 4 or more repair attempts OR vehicle is out of service for a cumulative total of 30 or more business days for any nonconformity.

CONSUMER PROCEDURES

Consumer must give written notice of the defect to the manufacturer or distributor, its agent or authorized dealer.

No provision is included for an additional repair opportunity.

Consumer must first utilize manufacturer's informal dispute resolution procedure if it complies with Magnuson-Moss.

AWARDS

If the consumer prevails, the manufacturer will be required to:
- Replace vehicle; OR
- Refund the original purchase price and all collateral charges.
    - Usage will be deducted based on consumer use of the vehicle prior to the first report of the nonconformity and during subsequent periods when the vehicle was not out of service for repair.

STATE CONTACT INFORMATION

State of New Hampshire
Consumer Protection and Antitrust Division
Office of the Attorney General
State House Annex
Concord, New Hampshire 03301
603/271-3641

NEW JERSEY

(Ch. 215-1983; 135-1984)

COVERAGE

Qualifying vehicles must:
- Be passenger vehicles registered by the Division of Motor Vehicles in Department of Law and Public Safety.
- Be purchased or leased in New Jersey or have ownership transferred during the express warranty period.

Coverage period is the earlier of:
- Two years OR 18,000 miles from original delivery.

Defect must substantially impair use, market value or safety.

Defect cannot result from alteration, abuse or neglect.

Nonconformity must continue to exist after 3 or more repair attempts OR vehicle is out of service for a cumulative total of 20 or more calendar days for one or more nonconformities.

CONSUMER PROCEDURES

Consumer must give written notice of the defect to the manufacturer, certified mail, return receipt requested.

Notice may be sent after vehicle has been serviced 2 times or out of service 20 or more calendar days. The final repair opportunity constitutes the third repair attempt.

Within 10 days of receipt of the notice, the manufacturer has an additional opportunity to repair the vehicle.

Consumer may utilize the dispute resolution system provided by the manufacturer OR Division of Consumer Affairs in the Department of Law and Public Safety OR seek redress through civil court. (Information on state program available at address below; $50.00 filing fee.)

Consumer is not required to use one mechanism prior to another.

AWARDS

If the consumer prevails, the manufacturer will be required to:
- Replace vehicle; OR
- Refund the original purchase price and all collateral charges including sales tax, preparation fees and other similar charges.
    - Usage will be deducted from both replacement/refund per the following formula:

$$\text{Contract Price} \times \frac{\text{\# Miles at First Repair}}{100{,}000}$$

- Note: If the consumer pays for repairs after one year/ 12,000 miles but within lemon law coverage, the consumer may recover those costs.

STATE CONTACT INFORMATION

State of New Jersey; Division of Consumer Affairs
1100 Raymond Boulevard, Room 504
Newark, NJ 07102
201/648-3135

I-41

NEW MEXICO

(57-16A-1 to 57-16A-9, NMSA 1978)

COVERAGE
Qualifying vehicles must:
- Be intended primarily for personal, family or household use.
- Be sold and registered in New Mexico or have ownership transferred during the express warranty period.

Coverage period is the earlier of:
- One year from delivery OR express warranty period.
- Action must be brought within 18 months of original delivery date or 90 days after final action of an informal dispute settlement mechanism.

Defect must substantially impair use and market value and render vehicle nonconforming to applicable warranty.

Defect cannot result from alteration, abuse or neglect.

Nonconformity must continue to exist after 4 or more repair attempts OR vehicle is out of service for a cumulative total of 30 or more business days for any nonconformity.

CONSUMER PROCEDURES
Consumer must give written notice of the defect to the manufacturer if the manufacturer has provided clear and conspicuous notice of this requirement.

The manufacturer is allowed one additional repair opportunity upon receipt of the written notice.

Consumer must first utilize manufacturer's informal dispute resolution procedure if it complies with Magnuson-Moss.

The state Attorney General may investigate and determine whether or not a procedure is fair, impartial and conforms to Magnuson-Moss.

AWARDS
If the consumer prevails, the manufacturer will be required to:
- Replace vehicle; OR
- Refund the original purchase price and all collateral charges including taxes, license/registration fees, other governmental charges.
    - Usage will be deducted from both replacement/refund based on consumer use prior to the first report of the nonconformity and during subsequent periods when the vehicle was not out of service for repair.
- Reasonable attorney's fees may be awarded in court action.

STATE CONTACT INFORMATION
State of New Mexico
Office of the Attorney General, Consumer Protection Division
P.O. Drawer 1508
Santa Fe, New Mexico 87504
505/827-6060; 1/800/432-2070 (Toll Free in New Mexico)

NEW YORK

(General Business Law, Sec. 198-a)

COVERAGE
Qualifying vehicles must:
- Be normally used for personal, family or household purposes.
- Be sold, leased or registered in New York.

Coverage period is the earlier of:
- Two years OR 18,000 miles from original delivery.
- An action must be initiated within 4 years of delivery.

Defect must substantially impair value to the consumer.

Defect cannot result from alteration, abuse or neglect.

Nonconformity must continue to exist after 4 or more repair attempts OR vehicle is out of service for a cumulative total of 30 or more calendar days for one or more nonconformities.

CONSUMER PROCEDURES
Consumer must give notice to the manufacturer, its agents or authorized dealer. (Statute does not state in writing.)

No additional repair attempt by the manufacturer required.

Consumer must utilize either manufacturer's informal dispute resolution procedure or state arbitration board prior to initiating court action. (Information on state arbitration board available through address below; $200 filing fee.)

AWARDS
If the consumer prevails, the manufacturer will be required to (at the consumer's option):
- Replace vehicle with a comparable new vehicle; OR
- Refund the original purchase price, sales tax (obtained from State Tax Commission on form provided by the manufacturer), license and registration, similar governmental charges.

- Usage can be deducted based on consumer use in excess of 12,000 miles per the following formula:

$$\frac{\text{Mileage Over 12,000}}{1} \times \frac{\text{Contract Price}}{100,000}$$

STATE CONTACT INFORMATION
State of New York
Office of the Attorney General
Bureau of Consumer Frauds
State Capitol
Albany, New York 12224
518/474-5481

(Consumers may also contact the nearest office of the Attorney General for information or to initiate arbitration through the state arbitration board.)

New York has also enacted a Lemon Law which covers used vehicles. This used vehicle Lemon Law has separate provisions from those outlined above. Consumers seeking information on the used vehicle Lemon Law should contact the Attorney General's Office for further information.

NORTH CAROLINA

(Ch. 385, Sec. 1)

COVERAGE
Qualifying vehicles must:
- Be intended primarily for use on public highways.
- Be purchased or leased in North Carolina.

Coverage period is the earlier of:
- One year from delivery OR express warranty period.
- Condition must occur not later than 24 months or 24,000 miles from original delivery.

Defect must substantially impair value to the consumer.

Defect cannot result from alteration, abuse or neglect.

Nonconformity must continue to exist after 4 or more repair attempts OR vehicle is out of service for a cumulative total of 20 or more calendar days during any 12 month period of the warranty for one or more nonconformities.

CONSUMER PROCEDURES

Consumer must give written notice of the defect to the manufacturer if the manufacturer has provided clear and conspicuous notice of this requirement.

The manufacturer is allowed one additional repair opportunity within 15 calendar days receipt of the written notice.

Consumer must first utilize manufacturer's informal dispute resolution procedure if it complies with Magnuson-Moss AND the manufacturer provides adequate written notice to the consumer about the procedure.

AWARDS

If the consumer prevails, the manufacturer will be required to
(at the consumer's option):
- Replace vehicle; OR
- Refund the original purchase price and all collateral charges including sales tax, license/registration fees, finance charges incurred after first report of the nonconformity, incidental costs, non-refundable portions of extended warranties and service contracts.
    - Usage will be deducted based on the following formula:

    $$\text{Contract Price} \times \frac{\text{\# Miles at Repurchase}}{100{,}000}$$

- Lessees will receive all sums paid entering into the lease agreement and incidental and consequential damages incurred less usage. Lessors will receive a full refund of lease price plus 5% of the lease price less 85% of the amount actually paid by the lessee.
- Treble damages may be awarded if manufacturer fails to comply; attorney's fees can be recovered if manufacturer unreasonably failed or refused to resolve matter.

STATE CONTACT INFORMATION

State of North Carolina
Office of the Attorney General, Consumer Protection Division
Department of Justice Building; P.O. Box 629
Raleigh, North Carolina 27602; 919/733-7741

---- ◆ ----

NORTH DAKOTA

(N.D. Century Code, Ch. 51-07)

COVERAGE
Qualifying vehicles must:
- Be intended primarily for personal, family or household purposes.
- Be purchased in North Dakota or have ownership transferred during the express warranty period.

Coverage period is the earlier of:
- One year from delivery OR express warranty period.
- An action must be brought within 6 months of the earlier of the express warranty or 18 months from delivery.

Defect must substantially impair use and market value.

Defect cannot result from alteration, abuse or neglect.

Nonconformity must continue to exist after 3 or more repair attempts OR vehicle is out of service for a cumulative total of 30 or more business days for any nonconformity.

CONSUMER PROCEDURES
Consumer must give written notice of the defect to the manufacturer.

The manufacturer is allowed one additional repair opportunity upon receipt of the written notice.

Consumer must first utilize manufacturer's informal dispute resolution procedure if it complies with Magnuson-Moss AND:
- The procedure is qualified (as determined by the state Attorney General); OR
- The manufacturer participates in a consumer/industry appeals, arbitration or mediation board with decisions binding upon the manufacturer.

AWARDS
If the consumer prevails, the manufacturer will be required to:
- Replace vehicle; OR
- Refund the original purchase price and all collateral charges.
    - Usage will be deducted for consumer use prior to the first report of the nonconformity and during subsequent periods when the vehicle was not out of service for repairs.
- Action initiated under this legislation precludes other legal remedies.

STATE CONTACT INFORMATION
State of North Dakota
Office of the Attorney General
State Capitol Building
600 E. Boulevard
Bismarck, North Dakota 58505
701/224-3404; 1/800/472-2600 (Toll Free in North Dakota)

OHIO

(Rev. Code Section 1345.71-1345.77)

COVERAGE
Qualifying vehicles must:
- Be passenger cars or non-commercial motor vehicles.
- Be owned or leased by an individual entitled to the terms of the manufacturer's warranty.

Coverage period is the earlier of:
- One year OR 18,000 miles from original delivery.
- An action must be brought within 2 years of the expiration of the express warranty period (may be extended pending decision of informal dispute resolution mechanism).

Defect must substantially impair use, market value or safety and render vehicle nonconforming to the warranty.

Defect cannot result from alteration, abuse or neglect.

Nonconformity must continue to exist after 3 or more repair attempts OR vehicle is out of service for a cumulative total of 30 or more calendar days OR vehicle has been subject to 8 or more repair attempts for any nonconformities that substantially impair the use or value OR at least 1 repair has been made and a nonconformity continues to exist which is likely to cause death or serious bodily injury.

CONSUMER PROCEDURES
The consumer must submit a demand for relief to the manufacturer.

No provision for an additional repair opportunity.

Consumer must first utilize manufacturer's informal dispute resolution procedure if it complies with Magnuson-Moss AND the manufacturer provides adequate written notice to the consumer about the procedure AND the program has been deemed to be "qualified" by the state.

AWARDS

If the consumer prevails, the manufacturer will be required to
(at the consumer's option):
- Replace vehicle; OR
- Refund the original purchase price including transportation, dealer-installed accessories, dealer services, preparation, delivery and all collateral charges including sales tax, license/registration fees, governmental charges, finance and credit insurance charges, warranty and service contract charges.
- If the manufacturer does not comply, consumer may bring a civil action and recover reasonable attorney's fees and court costs.

STATE CONTACT INFORMATION

State of Ohio
Office of the Attorney General; Consumer Frauds & Crimes Sect.
30 East Broad Street
State Office Tower, 25th Floor
Columbus, Ohio 43266-0410
614/466-4986; 1/800/282-0515; 614/466-1393 (TDD)

OKLAHOMA

(Okla. Stat. Ann. Title 15, Sec. 901)

COVERAGE

Qualifying vehicles must:
- Be motor driven vehicles purchased in Oklahoma or have ownership transferred during the express warranty.
- Be required to be registered in Oklahoma.

Coverage period is the earlier of:
- One year from delivery OR express warranty period.

Defect must substantially impair use and value.

Defect cannot result from alteration, abuse or neglect.

Nonconformity must continue to exist after 4 or more repair attempts OR vehicle is out of service for a cumulative total of 45 or more calendar days for reason of repair.

CONSUMER PROCEDURES

Consumer must give written notice of the defect to the manufacturer.

The manufacturer is allowed one additional repair opportunity upon receipt of the written notice.

Consumer must first utilize manufacturer's informal dispute resolution procedure if it complies with Magnuson-Moss.

AWARDS
If the consumer prevails, the manufacturer will be required to:
- Replace vehicle; OR
- Refund the original purchase price and all collateral charges including taxes, license/registration fees, similar governmental charges. (Interest is specifically excluded.)
- Usage will be deducted based on the first written report of the nonconformity and during subsequent periods when the vehicle was not out of service for repair.

STATE CONTACT INFORMATION
Oklahoma Attorney General
Consumer Protection Unit
112 State Capitol Building
Oklahoma City, Oklahoma 73105

Consumer Hotline: 405/524-4511
Attorney General's Office: 405/521-3921

OREGON

(ORS 646.315 to 646.375)

COVERAGE
Qualifying vehicles must:
- Be intended primarily for personal, family or household purposes.
- Be purchased or leased in Oregon or transferred for similar purposes during the express warranty period.

Coverage period is the earlier of:
- One year OR 12,000 miles from original delivery.
- Action must be brought within the earlier of 1 year from original delivery or the date on which the mileage reaches 12,000 miles on the odometer.

Defect must substantially impair use, market value or safety.

Defect cannot result from alteration, abuse or neglect.

Nonconformity must continue to exist after 4 or more repair attempts OR vehicle is out of service for a cumulative total of 30 or more business days for reasons of repair.

CONSUMER PROCEDURES
Consumer must give written notice of the defect to the manufacturer.

The manufacturer is allowed one additional repair opportunity upon receipt of the written notice.

Consumer must first utilize manufacturer's informal dispute resolution procedure if it complies with Magnuson-Moss AND the manufacturer provides adequate notice to consumer about availability of the procedure AND arbitration decision under the procedure is binding on the manufacturer.

AWARDS

If the consumer prevails, the manufacturer will be required to:
- Replace vehicle; OR
- Refund the original purchase or lease price and all collateral charges including sales tax, license fees, registration fees, similar collateral charges, excluding interest.
    - Usage will be deducted based on the first written report of the nonconformity and during subsequent periods when the vehicle was not out of service for repair.

STATE CONTACT INFORMATION

State of Oregon
Department of Justice
Justice Building
Salem Oregon 97310
503/378-4320 (9am - 1pm)

PENNSYLVANIA

(P.L. 150, No. 28)

COVERAGE

Qualifying vehicles must:
- Be used primarily for personal, family or household purposes.
- Be purchased and registered in Pennsylvania or have ownership transferred during the term of the warranty.

Coverage period is the earlier of:
- One year OR 12,000 miles from original delivery OR the term of the warranty.

Defect must substantially impair use, value or safety and render vehicle nonconforming to the warranty.

Defect cannot result from alteration, abuse or neglect.

Nonconformity must continue to exist after 3 or more repair attempts OR vehicle is out of service for a cumulative total of 30 or more calendar days for any nonconformity.

CONSUMER PROCEDURES

No provision for notice to manufacturer.

No provision for an additional repair opportunity.

Consumer must first utilize manufacturer's informal dispute resolution procedure if it complies with Magnuson-Moss AND the procedure is not binding upon the consumer.

AWARDS

If the consumer prevails, the manufacturer will be required to
(at the consumer's option):
- Replace vehicle with comparable vehicle of equal value; OR
- Refund the original purchase price and all collateral charges.
    - Usage will be deducted based on consumer use prior to the first report of the nonconformity at 10 cents per mile driven or 10 percent of the purchase price whichever is less.

STATE CONTACT INFORMATION

State of Pennsylvania
Office of the Attorney General; Bureau of Consumer Protection
Strawberry Square, 14th Floor
Harrisburg, Pennsylvania 17120
717/787-9707; 1/800/441-2555 (Toll Free in Pennsylvania)
717/787-7385 (Legislative Bureau)

RHODE ISLAND

(Chapter 31-5.2)

COVERAGE

Qualifying vehicles must:
- Be sold, leased registered or awarded as a replacement under this law in Rhode Island or have ownership transferred during the express warranty period.

Coverage period is the earlier of:
- One year OR 15,000 miles from original delivery.
- Action must be brought within the earlier of 3 years from original delivery or 2 years after date the odometer reaches 15,000 miles. (May be extended until 30 days after decision when a qualified dispute resolution procedure is being utilized.)

Defect must substantially impair use, market value or safety and render vehicle non-

I-51

conforming to the express or implied warranty.

Defect cannot result from alteration, abuse or neglect.

Nonconformity must continue to exist after 4 or more repair attempts OR vehicle is out of service for a cumulative total of 30 or more calendar days for any nonconformity.

CONSUMER PROCEDURES

No provision for notice to manufacturer.

The manufacturer has 7 calendar days to perform a final repair beginning on the day the manufacturer knows or should have known the lemon law provisions have been met or exceeded.

State arbitration, an automobile dispute settlement procedure administered by the Rhode Island Consumer's Council, is available to consumers who purchased a vehicle on or after 1/1/91. Information may be obtained through the address below; a $20.00 filing fee is assessed.

Consumers who purchase or lease vehicles after January 1, 1991 must use the manufacturer's informal dispute settlement procedure prior to the state arbitration procedure before initiating court action.

AWARDS

If the consumer prevails, the manufacturer will be required to
(at the consumer's option):
- Replace vehicle within 30 days including reimbursement for transfer of registration, sales tax and towing and car rental costs. (If financing is through the manufacturer or a subsidiary, consumer may not be required to enter into an agreement with a higher interest rate or unfavorable financial terms.) OR
- Refund the full contract price including credits and trade-in allowance, reimbursement for towing and car rental costs, reimbursement for incidental costs including sales tax, registration fees, finance charges, non-removable dealer options.
    - Usage will be deducted per the following formula:

$$\text{Contract Price} \times \frac{\text{\# Miles at First Report*}}{100{,}000}$$

* Also during subsequent periods when vehicle was not out of service for repair.
- Reasonable attorney's fees may be recovered in court action.

STATE CONTACT INFORMATION

State of Rhode Island; Consumer Protection Division
Department of the Attorney General
72 Pine Street
Providence, Rhode Island 02903

401/277-2104; 401/274-4400, ext. 354 (TDD)
800/852-7776 (Toll Free in Rhode Island)

Rhode Island Automobile Dealers Association
335-D Centerville Road
Warwick, Rhode Island 02886
401/732-6870
800/966-7423 (Toll Free in Rhode Island)

SOUTH CAROLINA

(Title 56, Ch. 28)

COVERAGE

Qualifying vehicles must:
- Be purchased or leased and normally used for personal, family or household purposes and subject to the manufacturer's express warranty.
- Be sold and registered in South Carolina.

Coverage period is the earlier of:
- One year OR 12,000 miles from original delivery.

Defect must substantially impair use, market value or safety.

Defect cannot result from alteration, abuse or neglect.

Nonconformity must continue to exist after 3 or more repair attempts OR vehicle is out of service for a cumulative total of 30 or more calendar days.

CONSUMER PROCEDURES

Consumer must give written notice of the defect to the manufacturer via registered, certified or express mail if the manufacturer has provided prominent notice of this requirement at the time of sale.

The manufacturer is allowed one additional repair opportunity upon receipt of the written notice.

The manufacturer shall notify consumer within 10 business days of a reasonably accessible repair facility and shall repair the vehicle within 10 days of delivery to the facility.

Consumer must first utilize manufacturer's informal dispute resolution procedure if it complies with Magnuson-Moss OR manufacturer participates in a consumer-industry appeals, arbitration or mediation panel whose decisions are binding on the manufacturer.

The state provides arbitration in those cases where the manufacturer does not offer a procedure which complies with Magnuson-Moss. Information is available through the address below.

AWARDS

If the consumer prevails, the manufacturer will be required to
(at the manufacturer's option):
- Replace vehicle; OR
- Refund the original purchase price and applicable finance charges, sales taxes, license/registration fees, other similar governmental charges.
    - Usage will be deducted based on the first report of the nonconformity per the following formula:

$$\text{Purchase Price} \times \frac{\text{\# Miles @ First Report}}{120,000}$$

STATE CONTACT INFORMATION

South Carolina Department of Consumer Affairs
P.O. Box 5757
Colubmia, South Carolina 29250
803/734-9452; 803/734-9455 (TDD)
800/922-1594 (Toll Free in South Carolina)

———————— ◆ ————————

SOUTH DAKOTA

No Lemon Law

———————— ◆ ————————

TENNESSEE

(Ch. 1004, Ch. 857)

COVERAGE

Qualifying vehicles must:
- Be intended primarily for personal, family or household use.
- Be sold or leased in Tennessee or have ownership transferred during the express warranty period.
- Be subject to registration requirements and have a Certificate of Title in Tennessee.

Coverage period is the earlier of:
- One year from delivery OR express warranty period.
- Action must be brought within 6 months of the later of the express warranty period or one year from original delivery.

Defect must substantially impair reliability, safety or market value and render vehicle nonconforming to applicable warranty.

Defect cannot result from alteration, abuse or neglect.

Nonconformity must continue to exist after 4 or more repair attempts OR vehicle is out of service for a cumulative total of 30 or more calendar days for reason of repair.

CONSUMER PROCEDURES

Consumer must give written notice of the defect to the manufacturer via certified mail.

The manufacturer is allowed one additional repair opportunity within 10 days of receipt of the written notice.

Consumer must first utilize manufacturer's informal dispute resolution procedure if it complies with Magnuson-Moss AND the mechanism provides notification of the procedure concerning refunds/replacement AND the Attorney General of Tennessee has issued a determination that the procedure qualifies as being in compliance.

AWARDS

If the consumer prevails, the manufacturer will be required to:
- Replace vehicle with a comparable new vehicle; OR
- Refund the original purchase price and all collateral charges including taxes, license/registration fees, title charges, manufacturer-installed or agent-installed items or service charges, credit life and disability insurance charges, other reasonable expenses incurred.
    - Usage will be deducted based on consumer use prior to the first report of the nonconformity and during subsequent periods when the vehicle was not out of service for repair not to exceed 1/2 the IRS allowance for use of a personal vehicle for business.

- Lessee shall receive aggregate deposit and rental payments less service fees and lessor shall receive the lease price less the deposit and rental payments for lease refunds.

STATE CONTACT INFORMATION

Division of Consumer Affairs
Department of Commerce & Insurance
500 James Robertson Parkway
Nashville, Tennessee 37219
615/741-4737
800/342-8385 (Toll Free in Tennessee)

TEXAS

(Tex. Rev. Civ. Stat. Ann. Art. 4413(36), Sec. 6.07)

COVERAGE

Qualifying vehicles must:
- Be new motor vehicles sold on or after 10/1/83 titled in Texas or any other state OR
- Be legally transferred during the period of the manufacturer's express warranty.
- Be owned by any person or entity entitled to the terms of the applicable warranty.

Coverage period is the earlier of*:
- One year from original delivery OR express warranty.
- Coverage may be extended if the consumer reports a defect to the manufacturer during the one year OR express warranty period and it is not resolved.
- An action must be initiated within 6 months of the earlier of the expiration of the express warranty or one year from original delivery.

Defect must substantially impair use and market value.

Defect cannot result from alteration, abuse or neglect.

Nonconformity must continue to exist after 4 or more repair attempts OR vehicle is out of service for a cumulative total of 30 or more calendar days for repair (out of service days for which the consumer is provided alternate transportation are not included).

CONSUMER PROCEDURES

Consumer must give written notice of the nonconformity to the manufacturer.

Manufacturer must be allowed one additional repair opportunity after receipt of the written notice.

Consumer may utilize either manufacturer's informal dispute resolution procedure OR pursue relief through Texas Motor Vehicle Commission (state-arbitration). Information on state arbitration board is available through address below.

Consumers who remain dissatisfied after utilizing the manufacturer's procedure may subsequently file a claim with Texas Motor Vehicle Commission.

AWARDS

If the consumer prevails, the manufacturer will be required to:
- Replace vehicle with a comparable new vehicle; OR
- Refund the full purchase price.
- Usage deduction for reasonable use per the following formula:

$$\text{Purchase Price} \times \frac{\text{\# Miles at First Report}}{100,000}$$

Plus 50% of the following:

$$\text{Purchase Price} \times \frac{\text{\# Miles At Date of Repurchase Award}}{100,000}$$

- Provisions for lease refunds not yet finalized by Texas.

STATE CONTACT INFORMATION

State of Texas; Texas Motor Vehicle Commission
Consumer Affairs Division
P.O. Box 2293
Austin, Texas 78768-2293
512/476-3618

* The Texas statute creates a presumption that a consumer is entitled to a refund/replacement if the vehicle meets the criteria described above. Under the terms of the law, if the manufacturer declines such a refund/replacement when demand is made by the consumer, it must be able to successfully "rebut" the presumption. This rebuttal can be based on the fact that the manufacturer was not provided with a reasonable number of repair opportunities; the defect did not substantially impair the vehicle; or the condition resulted from misuse, abuse, damage or improper maintenance.

If a consumer initiates action beyond the period described under "Length of Coverage" but within the warranty period, the consumer may still prevail. However, the burden of proof shifts from the manufacturer to the consumer and it is the consumer who must prove that a substantial nonconformity exists that has not been repaired in a reasonable number of attempts.

I-57

UTAH

(C. 1953, 13-20, enacted by L. 1985, Ch. 168, Sec. 1)

COVERAGE

Qualifying vehicles must:
- Be new motor vehicles sold in Utah or transferred during the express warranty.

Coverage period is the earlier of:
- Express warranty period OR one year from original delivery.

Defect must substantially impair use, market value or safety.

Defect cannot result from alteration, abuse or neglect.

Nonconformity must continue to exist after 4 or more repair attempts OR vehicle is out of service for a cumulative total of 30 or more business days because of repairs.

CONSUMER PROCEDURES

No requirement for notice to manufacturer.

No requirement for an additional repair opportunity by the manufacturer.

Consumer must first utilize manufacturer's informal dispute resolution procedure if it complies with Magnuson-Moss.

AWARDS

If the consumer prevails, the manufacturer will be required to:
- Replace vehicle with a comparable vehicle; OR
- Refund the original purchase price and all collateral charges.
    - Usage will be deducted for mileage directly attributable to consumer use prior to first report of nonconformity and during any subsequent periods when vehicle was not out of service for repairs.

STATE CONTACT INFORMATION

State of Utah
Office of the Attorney General
Department of Consumer Protection
160 E. 3rd South
Salt Lake City, Utah 84145
801/530-6601

VERMONT

(Act 211, 9 V.S.A., Ch. 115, No. 260)

COVERAGE

Qualifying vehicles must:
- Be purchased, leased or registered in Vermont and registered within 15 days of purchase or have ownership transferred during the express warranty.
- If leased, have a lease term of at least two years.
- Be new motor vehicles, including demonstrators.

Coverage period is the express warranty period.
- An action must be initiated within 1 year of the later of the expiration of the express warranty or the manufacturer's last attempt to repair the nonconformity.

Defect must substantially impair use, market value or safety and must render vehicle nonconforming to the warranty.

Defect cannot result from alteration, abuse or neglect.

Nonconformity must continue to exist after 3 or more repair attempts OR vehicle is out of service for a cumulative total of 30 or more calendar days for one or more nonconformities.

Repair attempts must be documented by a written statement of work performed and applies only if the repair attempts are by the same dealer unless good cause is shown for taking the vehicle to another dealer.

CONSUMER PROCEDURES

Consumer must give written notice of the nonconformity to the manufacturer and indicate on forms provided by the manufacturer at time of sale if he/she chooses arbitration under the state program or the manufacturer's program.
- Manufacturer must be allowed one additional repair opportunity after receipt of the written notice.
- Consumer may utilize either manufacturer's informal dispute resolution procedure OR pursue relief through the state program.
- Information on state arbitration board is available through address below.
- Both programs are obligated to resolve the matter within 45 days.
- The consumer's choice of one procedure precludes his/her right to pursue the other method.
- A consumer may also pursue redress through civil court without first pursuing informal dispute resolution.

AWARDS

If the consumer prevails, the manufacturer will be required to
(at the consumer's option):
- Replace vehicle with a comparable new vehicle; OR
- Refund the full purchase price and all collateral charges including registration/ license fees, credits, trade-in allowances/down payments, finance and credit charges, incidental and consequential damages (purchase and use tax is refunded by the Commissioner of Motor Vehicles).
- Lessees receive the aggregate deposit and rental payments made to the lessor and incidental and consequential damages.
- Usage deduction for reasonable use per the following formula based on use prior to first repair:

$$\text{Contract Price} \times \frac{\text{\# Miles at First Repair}}{100,000}$$

STATE CONTACT INFORMATION

State of Vermont
Office of Consumer Protection
Office of the Attorney General
109 State Street
Montpelier, Vermont 05602
802/828-3171

Motor Vehicle Arbitration Board
118 State Street
Montpelier, Vermont 05602
802/828-2669

VIRGINIA

(Ch. 773; Ch. 603)

COVERAGE

Qualifying vehicles must:
- Be used substantially for personal, family or household purposes.

Coverage period is eighteen months from original delivery. (May be extended if the manufacturer has been notified during this period but the defect has not been corrected.)

Defect must substantially impair use, market value or safety and render the vehicle nonconforming to the warranty.

I-60

Defect cannot result from alteration, abuse or neglect.

Nonconformity must continue to exist after 3 or more repair attempts OR vehicle is out of service for a cumulative total of 30 or more calendar days due to repairs OR 1 or more repair attempts do not correct a nonconformity which is a serious safety defect.

CONSUMER PROCEDURES

Consumer must give written notice to the manufacturer if this requirement was clearly and conspicuously disclosed by the manufacturer, including the proper address. (This provision applies unless manufacturer's representative has inspected vehicle and recommended corrective measures which failed to correct the nonconformity.)

The manufacturer is allowed 1 additional repair attempt within 15 days of receipt of the notice.

It is the consumer's option whether to utilize the manufacturer's procedure prior to pursuing other redress.

AWARDS

If the consumer prevails, the manufacturer will be required to
(at the consumer's option):
- Replace vehicle with an acceptable comparable vehicle; OR
- Refund the original purchase price and all collateral charges including sales tax, license/registration fees, title fees, finance charges and interest, dealer preparation charges and charges for service contracts, undercoating, rust proofing and installed options not recoverable from a third party, incidental damages as defined by the Uniform Commercial Code.
    - Usage will be deducted based on 1/2 the amount per mile allowed by the IRS for business use of a personal vehicle.

STATE CONTACT INFORMATION

State of Virginia
Division of Consumer Affairs
Post Office Box 1163
Richmond, VA 23209
804/786-2042; 800/552-9963 (Toll Free in Virginia)

WASHINGTON

(RCW 19.118)

COVERAGE

Qualifying vehicles must:
- Be self-propelled vehicles designed primarily for highway use.
- Be leased or purchased and registered in Washington.

Coverage period is the earlier of:
- Two years OR 24,000 miles from original delivery date.
- Manufacturers must submit to arbitration for a period of 30 months from delivery if the state board accepts the case.

Defect must substantially impair use, value or safety.

Defect cannot result from alteration, abuse or neglect.

Nonconformity must continue to exist after 4 or more repair attempts OR vehicle is out of service for a cumulative total of 30 or more calendar days during which the repair shop is open for one or more nonconformities OR 2 or more repair attempts for serious safety defect and the nonconformity is not corrected.

CONSUMER PROCEDURES

Consumer must give notice of the nonconformity to the manufacturer.

No requirement to allow manufacturer an additional repair opportunity.

Consumer may utilize either manufacturer's informal dispute resolution procedure OR pursue relief through the state board but must utilize an informal dispute resolution mechanism prior to initiating court action. Information on state arbitration board is available through address below.

AWARDS

If the consumer prevails, the manufacturer will be required to
(at the consumer's option):
- Replace vehicle with an identical or reasonably equivalent new vehicle and the consumer will pay a usage deduction; OR
- Refund the full purchase price and collateral charges including sales tax, registration/license fees, finance charges, arbitration service fees, prepayment penalties, credit disability and credit life insurance charges not otherwise refundable, any other insurance costs prorated for time out of service, transportation and dealer preparation charges, service contract charges, undercoating, rustproofing and factory or dealer installed options and incidental costs such as towing and rental vehicle costs.

- Usage deduction for reasonable use per the following formula based on number of miles prior to acceptance for repurchase:

$$\frac{\text{Mileage at Return}}{} \times \frac{\text{Purchase Price}}{100,000}$$

- Lessees will receive all payments made under the lease including all payments, trade-in value or inception payment, security deposit, all collateral charges as defined above and incidental costs as defined above. A usage deduction will be charged to the consumer. In addition, the lessor and/or lienholder will receive all payment necessary to secure title to the vehicle and relieve the lessee of any obligation.

STATE CONTACT INFORMATION

State of Washington
Lemon Law Administrator; Attorney General's Office
1300 Dexter Horton Building
Seattle, Washington 98104
206/587-4240; 800/541-8898

———————— ◇ ————————

WEST VIRGINIA

(Article 6A, Chapter 46a)

COVERAGE

Qualifying vehicles must:
- Be used primarily for personal, family or household purposes.
- Be purchased and registered in West Virignia or transferred during the express warranty.

Coverage period is the earlier of:
- Express warranty period OR one year from original delivery.
- If defect was discovered during the term of the warranty or within one year from original delivery but repairs were not completed at that time, the manufacturer shall remain responsible.

Defect must substantially impair use or market value and render vehicle nonconforming to the warranty.

Defect cannot result from alteration, abuse or neglect.

Nonconformity must continue to exist after 3 or more repair attempts OR vehicle is out of service for a cumulative total of 30 or more calendar days for reason of repairs during the earlier of the express warranty period or one year from original delivery.

I-63

One repair attempt <u>may</u> qualify if the nonconformity is likely to cause death or serious bodily injury.

CONSUMER PROCEDURES

Consumer must given written notice of the defect to the manufacturer.

The manufacturer is allowed one additional repair opportunity unless the defect is likely to result in injury or death.

Consumer must first utilize manufacturer's informal dispute resolution procedure if it complies with Magnuson-Moss AND the manufacturer provides adequate written notice about the procedure AND the procedure has been approved by the West Virginia Attorney General's office.

AWARDS

If the consumer prevails, the manufacturer will be required to:
- Replace vehicle with a comparable vehicle.
- In the event the manufacturer fails to provide a replacement vehicle, the civil court can award a refund of the purchase price plus incidental expenses and attorney's fees. In a refund award, "reasonable" charges for useage may be deducted.

STATE CONTACT INFORMATION

State of West Virginia
Office of the Attorney General; Consumer Protection Division
812 Quarrier Street, 6th Floor
Charleston, West Virginia 25301
304/348-8986; 800/368-8808 (West Virginia only)

WISCONSIN

(Wisc. Statute 218.015)

COVERAGE

Qualifying vehicles must:
- Be new motor vehicles sold or leased in Wisconsin or have ownership transferred during the express warranty.

Coverage period is the earlier of:
- Express warranty period OR one year from original delivery.

Defect must substantially impair use, value or safety and render the vehicle nonconforming to the warranty.

Defect cannot result from alteration, abuse or neglect.

Nonconformity must continue to exist after 4 or more repair attempts OR vehicle is out of service for a cumulative total of 30 or more calendar days for repair of any nonconformities.

CONSUMER PROCEDURES

No notice to manufacturer is required.

No provision for an additional repair attempt by the manufacturer.

Consumer must first utilize manufacturer's informal dispute resolution procedure if it complies with Magnuson-Moss OR provides protection which is equal or greater to Magnuson-Moss AND has been certified by the state of Wisconsin.

AWARDS

If the consumer prevails, the manufacturer will be required to
(at the consumer's option):
- Replace vehicle with a comparable new vehicle and refund collateral costs; OR
- Refund the original purchase price and all collateral charges including sales tax, finance charges, amount paid by the consumer at point of sale, repair expenses including alternate transportation.
- Usage will be deducted only on refunds per the following formula:

$$\text{Contract Price} \times \frac{\text{\# Miles at First Report}}{100,000}$$

STATE CONTACT INFORMATION

State of Wisconsin 608/266-1852
Department of Justice 800/362-8189 (Toll Free in Wisconsin)
Office of Consumer Protection
P.O. Box 7856
Madison, Wisconsin 53707

WYOMING

(Wyo. Stat. 40-17-101; Ch. 54)

COVERAGE

Qualifying vehicles must:
- Be new, self-propelled motor vehicles.
- Be sold or registered in Wyoming and have express warranty coverage.

Coverage period is one year from original delivery.

Defect must substantially impair use and fair market value and render the vehicle nonconforming to the warranty.

Defect cannot result from alteration, abuse or neglect.

Nonconformity must continue to exist after 4 or more repair attempts OR vehicle is out of service for a cumulative total of 30 or more business days due to repair.

CONSUMER PROCEDURES

Consumer must give written notice to the manufacturer or the defect.

The manufacturer is allowed one additional opportunity to repair upon receipt of the written notice.

Consumer must first utilize manufacturer's informal dispute resolution procedure if it complies with Magnuson-Moss.

AWARDS

If the consumer prevails, the manufacturer will be required to:
- Replace vehicle with a comparable new vehicle of the same type, similarly equipped; OR
- Refund the original purchase price and all collateral charges.
- Usage will be deducted for use directly attributable to the consumer prior to the first report of the nonconformity and during subsequent periods when the vehicle was not out of service for repair.

STATE CONTACT INFORMATION

State of Wyoming
Office of the Attorney General
123 State Capitol Building
Cheyenne, Wyoming 82002
307/777-7841 or 777-6286

APPENDIX II

AUTOMOTIVE MANUFACTURER CONTACT INFORMATION

AUTHOR'S NOTE: This Appendix is intended to provide information for major automotive manufacturers. Every possible effort has been made to insure its accuracy, however, changes may have occurred since publication.

Listings provide contact information for each manufacturer's national office. If you wish to contact a manufacturer's zone or regional office, call or write the national office for information. You can also obtain contact information for the manufacturer of your automobile from the owner's manual provided with your vehicle, or from your dealership.

AUTOMOTIVE MANUFACTURERS

Name	Page
Alfa Romeo, Inc.	II-4
American Honda Motor Company, Inc.	II-4
• Acura Division	
American Isuzu Motors, Inc.	II-5
American Suzuki Motor Corporation	II-5
Audi of America, Inc.	II-5
BMW of North America, Inc.	II-6
Chrysler Motors Corporation	II-6
• Chrylser	
• Dodge	
• Eagle	
• Jeep	
• Plymouth	
Daihatsu	II-6
Fiat Auto, U.S.A., Inc.	II-7
Ford Motor Company	II-7
General Motors Corporation:	
• Buick Division	II-8
• Cadillac Division	II-8
• Chevrolet Division	II-8
• GMC Truck and Coach Division	II-9
• Oldsmobile Division	II-9
• Pontiac Division	II-10
Hyundai Motor America	II-10
Jaguar Cars, Inc.	II-10
Lotus Cars, U.S.A., Inc.	II-11
Maserati Automobiles, Inc.	II-11
Mazda Motors of America	II-11
Mercedes-Benz of North America, Inc.	II-11

Name	Page
Mitsubishi Motor Sales of America, Inc.	II-12
Nissan Motor Corporation in U.S.A.	II-12
• Infiniti Division	
Peugeot Motors of America, Inc.	II-13
Porsche Cars North America, Inc.	II-13
Rolls-Royce Motor Cars, Inc.	II-13
Saab-Scania of America, Inc.	II-14
Saturn	II-14
Sterling Motor Cars	II-14
Subaru of America, Inc.	II-15
Toyota Motor Sales, U.S.A., Inc.	II-15
• Lexus Division	
Volkswagen United States, Inc.	II-16
Volvo Cars of North America	II-16
Yugo America, Inc.	II-16

ALFA ROMEO, INC.

ARBITRATION PROGRAM: AUTOCAP

NATIONAL OFFICE:
Owner Relations Department
Alfa Romeo Distributors of
North America 8529 Exchange Drive
P.O. Box 598026
Orlando, FL 32859-8026
407/856-5070 or 856-5069
407/856-5075 (Fax)

AMERICAN HONDA MOTOR CO. INC.

ARBITRATION PROGRAM: AUTOLINE

NATIONAL OFFICE:
National Customer Affairs
Representative
American Honda Motor Co., Inc.
P.O. Box 50
100 W. Alondra Boulevard
Gardena, CA 90247
213/604-2430
800/521-1613

ACURA DIVISION

ARBITRATION PROGRAM: AUTOCAP/AUTOLINE

NATIONAL OFFICE:
National Customer Relations Department
Acura Division
American Honda Motor Co., Inc.
P.O. Box 50
100 W. Alondra Boulevard
Gardena, CA 90247
213/327-8280
800/382-2238

AMERICAN ISUZU MOTORS, INC.

ARBITRATION PROGRAM: AUTOCAP (Where Required/Case-By-Case Basis)

NATIONAL OFFICE: National Customer Relations Manager
American Isuzu Motors, Inc.
2300 Pellissier Place
Whittier, CA 90601
213/949-0611
800/255-6727

AMERICAN SUZUKI MOTOR CORPORATION

ARBITRATION PROGRAM: None

NATIONAL OFFICE: Customer Relations Department
American Suzuki Motor Corporation
Automotive Division
3251 E. Imperial Highway
Brea, CA 92621
1-800-877-6900

AUDI OF AMERICA, INC.

ARBITRATION PROGRAM: AUTOLINE

NATIONAL OFFICE: Customer Relations Manager
Audi of America, Inc.
888 W. Big Beaver Road
P.O. Box 3951
Troy, MI 48007-3951
1-800-822-2834
313/362-7300

BMW OF NORTH AMERICA, INC.

ARBITRATION PROGRAM: AUTOCAP (Case-by-Case Basis)
AUTOLINE (Minnesota)

NATIONAL OFFICE: Customer Relations Manager
BMW of North America, Inc.
300 Chestnut Ridge Rd.
P.O. Box 1227
Woodcliff Lake, NJ 07675
201/307-4000

CHRYSLER MOTORS CORPORATION
(Includes Chrylser, Dodge, Eagle, Jeep, Maserati, Plymouth)

ARBITRATION PROGRAM: Chrysler Customer Arbitration Board
(Jeeps manufactured prior to 88 model year are covered under AUTOLINE.)

NATIONAL OFFICE: National Owner Relations Manager
Chrysler Motors Corporation
P.O. Box 1718
Detroit, MI 48288-1718
1-800-992-1997
313/956-5970

DAIHATSU

ARBITRATION PROGRAM: Autosolve Complaint Arbitration Services, Inc.

NATIONAL OFFICE: Daihatsu America, Inc.
4422 Corporate Center Drive
Los Alamitos, CA 90270
714/761-7000

FIAT AUTO USA, INC.

ARBITRATION PROGRAM: AUTOCAP

NATIONAL OFFICE:
National Customer Relations Manager
Fiat Auto USA, Inc.
777 Terrace Avenue
Hasbrouck Heights, NJ 07604
201/393-4000

FORD MOTOR COMPANY

ARBITRATION PROGRAM: Ford Consumer Appeals Board
(1-800-392-3673)

NATIONAL OFFICE:
Manager, Owner Relations Department
Ford Motor Company
P.O. Box 1805
Dearborn, MI 48121
313/446-5880
800/255-1433

TOLL FREE NUMBERS:
Lincoln: 1-800-521-4140
Merkur: 1-800-437-8237
Tarus/Sable: 1-800-551-5747
Towing/Technical Info:
1-800-282-0959

BUICK (GENERAL MOTORS)

ARBITRATION PROGRAM: AUTOLINE

NATIONAL OFFICE:

Buick Customer Assistance Center
902 E. Hamilton Avenue
Flint, MI 48550
1-800-521-7300

CADILLAC (GENERAL MOTORS)

ARBITRATION PROGRAM: AUTOLINE

NATIONAL OFFICE:

Cadillac Customer Relations Center
2860 Clark Street
Detroit, MI 48232
1-800-458-8006

CHEVROLET (GENERAL MOTORS)

ARBITRATION PROGRAM: AUTOLINE

NATIONAL OFFICE:

Chevrolet/GEO Motor Division
Customer Assistance Department
P.O. Box 7047
Troy, MI 48009-7047
1-800-222-1020
1-800-TD-BUICK (TDD and TTY)

GMC TRUCK AND COACH DIVISION (GENERAL MOTORS)

ARBITRATION PROGRAM: AUTOLINE

CENTRAL OFFICE: GMC Truck Division
Customer Service Department
31 Judson Street
Pontiac, MI 48058
313/456-4547

OLDSMOBILE (GENERAL MOTORS)

ARBITRATION PROGRAM: AUTOLINE

NATIONAL OFFICE: Oldsmobile Division
Customer Service Department
P. O. Box 30095
Lansing, MI 48909-7595
517/ 377-5546
800-222-5566
1-800-TD-BUICK (TDD and TTY)

(NOTE: The Oldsmobile Division is in the process of establishing centralized customer service at the 800# listed above. It is currently available in most states and will be available nation-wide by the end of 1990.)

PONTIAC (GENERAL MOTORS)

ARBITRATION PROGRAM: AUTOLINE

NATIONAL OFFICE:
Pontiac Customer Assistance Center
One Pontiac Plaza
Pontiac, MI 48053
1-800-762-2737
1-800-TD-BUICK (TDD and TTY)

HYUNDAI MOTOR AMERICA

ARBITRATION PROGRAM: Autosolve Complaint Arbitration Services, Inc.

NATIONAL OFFICE:
National Consumer Affairs
Hyundai Motor America
10550 Talbert Avenue
Fountain Valley, CA 92728-0850
714/965-3009

JAGUAR CARS, INC.

ARBITRATION PROGRAM: AUTOCAP

NATIONAL OFFICE:
National Customer Relations Department
Jaguar Cars, Inc.
555 McArthur Boulevard
Mahwah, New Jersey 07430
201/818-8500

LOTUS CARS, USA, INC.

ARBITRATION PROGRAM: Autoline

NATIONAL OFFICE:
Lotus Cars, USA, Inc.
1655 Lakes Parkway
Lawrenceville, GA 30243
404/822-4566

MASERATI

ARBITRATION PROGRAM: None

NATIONAL OFFICE:
Maserati Automobiles, Inc.
1501 Caton Avenue
Baltimore, MD 21227
301/646-6400

MAZDA MOTOR OF AMERICA, INC.
ARBITRATION PROGRAM: AUTOCAP

NATIONAL OFFICE:
National Customer Relations Department
Mazda Motors of America, Inc.
7755 Irvine Center Drive
Irvine, CA 92718
714/727-1990
1-800-222-5500

MERCEDES-BENZ

ARBITRATION PROGRAM: None

NATIONAL OFFICE:
Owner Service Department
Mercedes-Benz of North America, Inc.
One Mercedes Drive
Montvale, NJ 07645
201/573-0600
201/573-2501

MITSUBISHI MOTOR SALES OF AMERICA, INC.

ARBITRATION PROGRAM: AUTOCAP

NATIONAL OFFICE:
Manager, Consumer Relations
Mitsubishi Motor Sales of America, Inc.
6400 W. Katella Avenue
Cypress, CA 90630
800/222-0037
714-372-6000

NISSAN MOTOR CORPORATION IN U.S.A.

ARBITRATION PROGRAM: AUTOCAP/AUTOLINE

NATIONAL OFFICE:
National Consumer Affairs Department
Nisson Motor Corporation in U.S.A
18501 S. Figueroa Street
Carson, CA 90248
1-800-647-7261

INFINITY (NISSAN)

ARBITRATION PROGRAM: AUTOCAP/AUTOLINE

NATIONAL OFFICE:
National Consumer Affairs Department
Infiniti Division
18701 S. Figueroa Street
Carson, CA 90248
1-800-662-6200

PEUGEOT MOTORS OF AMERICA, INC.

ARBITRATION PROGRAM: AUTOLINE (Available in California, Oregon, Minnesota and Kentucky)

NATIONAL OFFICE:
National Customer Relations Manager
Peugeot Motors of America, Inc.
One Peugeot Plaza
P.O. Box 607
Lyndhurst, NJ 07021
201/935-8400
1-800-345-5549

PORSCHE CARS NORTH AMERICA, INC.

ARBITRATION PROGRAM: American Arbitration Association

NATIONAL OFFICE:
Porsche Customer Service
Porsche Cars North America, Inc.
100 W. Liberty Street
P.O. Box 30911
Reno, NV 89520-3911
702/348-3154
800/255-5177

ROLLS-ROYCE MOTOR CARS, INC.

ARBITRATION PROGRAM: AUTOCAP

NATIONAL OFFICE:
Field Service Manager
Rolls-Royce Motor Cars, Inc.
P.O. Box 476
Lyndhurst, NJ 07071
201/460-9600

SAAB-SCANIA OF AMERICA, INC.

ARBITRATION PROGRAM: AUTOLINE

NATIONAL OFFICE:
Consumer Relations Manager
Saab-Scania of America, Inc.
P.O. Box 697
Orange, CT 06477
203/795-5671
1-800-548-1156 (toll free in CT)
1-800-255-9007 (toll free in U.S.)

SATURN

ARBITRATION PROGRAM: AUTOLINE

NATIONAL OFFICE:
Highway 31 South
Springhill, TN 37174
1-800-522-5000 (General Information)
1-800-553-6000 (Owner Assistance)

STERLING MOTOR CARS

ARBITRATION PROGRAM: AUTOCAP
BETTER BUSINESS BUREAU-
AUTOLINE (SOME STATES)

NATIONAL OFFICE:
Customer Relations Manager
Sterling Motor Cars
8953 N.W. 23rd Street
Miami, FL 33172
305/477-7400

SUBARU OF AMERICA, INC.

ARBITRATION PROGRAM: AUTOSOLVE Complaint Arbitration Services

NATIONAL OFFICE: National Owner Service Department
Subaru of America, Inc.
Subaru Plaza
P.O. Box 6000
Cherry Hill, NJ 08035
609/488-8500

TOYOTA MOTOR SALES, U.S.A., INC.

ARBITRATION PROGRAM: Autosolve Complaint Arbitration Services, Inc.

NATIONAL OFFICE: Customer Assistance Center
Toyota Motor Sales, U.S.A., Inc.
Department A404
19001 S. Western Avenue
Torrance, California 90509
1-800-331-4331

LEXUS DIVISION (TOYOTA)

ARBITRAITON PROGRAM: Autosolve Complaint Arbitration Services, Inc.

NATIONAL OFFICE: Lexus
A Division of Toyota Motor Sales, U.S.A., Inc.
Customer Satisfaction Department
P.O. Box 2991
Torrance, CA 90509-2991
1-800-255-3987

VOLKSWAGEN UNITED STATES, INC.

ARBITRATION PROGRAM: AUTOLINE

NATIONAL OFFICE: Customer Relations Manager
Volkswagen United States, Inc.
888 W. Big Beaver Road
P.O. Box 3951
Troy, MI 48007
1-800-822-8987
313/429-8100

VOLVO CARS OF NORTH AMERICA

ARBITRATION PROGRAM: (Only Available if Required by State Law)

NATIONAL OFFICE: Consumer Affairs Manager
Volvo Cars of North America
P.O. Box 914
Rockleigh, NJ 07647
201/767-4737

YUGO AMERICA, INC.

ARBITRATION PROGRAM: AUTOCAP

NATIONAL OFFICE: Manager, Customer Service
Yugo America, Inc.
28 Park Way
Upper Saddle River, NJ 07458
201/825-4600

APPENDIX III

ARBITRATION PROGRAM CONTACT INFORMATION

GOVERNMENTAL AGENCY CONTACT INFORMATION

ARBITRATION PROGRAM CONTACT INFORMATION

American Arbitration Association
140 West 51st Street
New York, New York 10020
212/484-4000

Autosolve Complaint Arbitration Services, Inc.
American Automobile Association
1000 AAA Drive
Heathrow, Florida 32746-5064
407/444-7740
1-800-47-SOLVE

Automotive Consumer Action Program (AUTOCAP)
8400 Westpark Drive
McLean, Virginia 22102
703/821-7144

BBB Auto Line
Council of Better Business Bureaus
4200 Wilson Boulevard
Suite 800
Arlington, Virginia 22203
703/276-0100
1-800-955-5100

Chrysler Customer Arbitration Board
P.O. Box 1718
Detroit, MI 48288
313/956-5970
1-800-992-1997

Ford Consumer Appeals Board
P.O. Box 1805
Dearborn, MI 48126
800/241-8450
1-800-392-3673

III-3

GOVERNMENTAL AGENCY CONTACT INFORMATION

National Highway Traffic
Safety Administration (NHTSA)
Department of Transportation
Washington, D.C. 20690
202/366-0123
202/755-8919 (TDD)
800/424-9393 (Toll Free)
800/424-9153 (Toll Free TDD)

AUTO SAFETY HOTLINE

- Provides information on recalls
- Accepts consumer complaints
- Investigates certain complaints

Federal Trade Commission
Correspondence Branch
Washington, D.C. 20580

- Investigates claims on trade practices

Public Reference Branch
Washington, D.C. 20580

- Provides information to consumers

INDEX

arbitration
    manufacturer, 14, 17, 31, 35
    state, 29, 32, 37
arbitration program contact
    information, Appendix III
awards, 17
automotive manufacturer contact
    information, Appendix II
civil court, 29, 33, 39
    process described, 39
    provisions of action, 33
competition, automotive industry, 4
complaints
    to dealer, 23
    to manufacturer, 25
    resolution with dealer, 24
    resolution with manufacturer, 26
consumerism, 5
coverage, length of, 15
days out of repair, 16
days out of service, 16
demand letter, 27, 29
    sample, 30
eligibility, 16
express limited warranty, 13
Federal Trade Commission, 14
FTC, 14
FTC rule 703, 10, 14
governmental agency contact
information, Appendix III
Lemon Law
    defined, 12-13
    explained, 13
    provisions (list), 15
    state-by-state laws, Appendix I
    step-by-step processes, 34-40
informal dispute settlement
    mechanism, 14, 17, 31, 35
    process described, 35
leased vehicles, 18
Magnuson-Moss Warranty Act, 2, 9, 15
maintenance records, 20
manufacturer's arbitration, 14, 17, 31, 35
    process described, 35
    provisions of action, 31
manufacturer's informal dispute
    settlement mechanism, 14, 17, 31, 35
    process described, 35
    provisions of action, 31
mileage deduction, 17
nonconformity, 14
notification, 28
prior resort, 32
procedures, consumer, 16
qualifying nonconformity, 16
qualifying vehicles, 15
recordskeeping, 20
repair attempt, 14
service records, 20-21
state arbitration, 29, 32, 37
    provisions of action, 32
state laws, Appendix I
warranty
    express limited, 13
    implied, 14